Whispers from Heaven

Whispers from Heaven

Volume One

Jeff Odell

FORWARD BY

Evangelist, Missionary, and Mentor

Dale Hathorn

STANDING TALL MINISTRIES

Inspiring Voices®
A Service of **Guideposts**

Inspiring Voices books may be ordered through booksellers or by contacting:

Inspiring Voices
1663 Liberty Drive
Bloomington, IN 47403
www.inspiringvoices.com
1-(866) 697-5313

Library of Congress Control Number: 2012917093

ISBN: 978-1-4624-0317-2 (sc)
ISBN: 978-1-4624-0316-5 (e)

Printed in the United States of America

Inspiring Voices rev. date: 10/02/2012

Table of Contents

FORWARD

A NUMBER OF YEARS AGO I served as the preacher for the New Prospect Camp Meeting near Vancleave, MS. As I was exiting the open-air tabernacle one evening, greeting different congregants along the way, I found myself led to a rather large-sized man standing in one of the rear, center rows of pews. As I approached him and introduced myself, I realized very quickly that he and I were of like stature, but also of like spirit. He was kind, gentle, and hungry for a deeper relationship with the Lord. After visiting for quite some time, we had an opportunity to pray together, and the Holy Spirit fell on Jeff Odell in a powerful and fresh way. It was from that night on, that he and I became good friends and closely connected in a God-relationship.

I had the privilege of speaking into Jeff's life on numerous occasions, and as I would find myself in ministry in other churches on the Mississippi Gulf Coast, it was not uncommon to see Jeff and various members of his family in the congregation. I heard the cries of his heart as he sought so diligently to walk in the power of the Holy Spirit. I wrestled with him through his call to ministry and ultimately his ordination.

Because of the miles that separate us geographically, Jeff and I have not been able to maintain the kind of relationship that both of us probably would have desired, but when God knits two people's hearts to each other, the bond is not quickly broken. I guess you could say, Jeff and I are joined.

As I have observed his life, I have seen Jeff go to the mountain tops and even soar like the eagle. I have also seen him in the deepest of valleys with very little energy left to climb. I realized though, that no matter what Jeff has faced, he has been constantly in love with a real Jesus, who has ministered to him, and whom Jeff has allowed to minister through him to others. Jeff started sending text messages a few years ago to encourage the recipients. Not knowing what any one individual might be going through, he still would send them, only to hear testimonies such as "that was just exactly what I needed today." Jeff has continued to send those "sayings" of the day. I know I have received them without fail, regardless of whether I was at home or in another country on the other side of the world.

Now the Lord has opened the door for him to share these messages through the printed page. I know that many will be blessed and encouraged as they read these writings. Know that the author is sharing them from his own heart of genuine love of God and compassion for you. As you read, it is my prayer that you allow the Holy Spirit who inspired Jeff Odell, to also stir in your own heart, lift your load, brighten your day, and lead you straight to the foot of the cross, where Jesus Christ gave Himself without reservation for you.

Yours in Christ,

Dale Hathorn
Standing Tall Ministries
Evangelist, Missionary, and Mentor

WHISPERS FROM HEAVEN

PREFACE

L ET ME START BY welcoming you to "Whispers from Heaven." The hope and goal of this book is to help all of us gain a closer walk and relationship with our Lord and Savior Jesus Christ. No matter how long any of us have had a relationship with Jesus or how devoted we may have been, each one of us can undoubtedly be closer. Jesus' desire is to be the very essence of each one of our lives. It is His desire to be our first waking thought, such as "What do you got for me today Lord?" Throughout our days there is nothing that can be any more refreshing than a quiet conversation with Jesus. Times when major events take place, talking with our Lord can give us an understanding and perspective that there is a greater plan in place and all will be well. Giving thanks at meals for what the Lord has provided for us, makes the meal taste a little bit better. Finally at night when our day's work is done, nothing brings a more warm and peaceful sleep than our last conversation of the day being with our Lord. The closer we walk with Jesus each day, the more we can be sure of every step we take.

The Whispers from Heaven started five years ago when I started texting an inspired message a couple times a week to friends and family.

The list quickly grew to over a hundred people a day receiving the text directly from me and many of those I sent it to were forwarding it on to their friends and family. During the first couple years of the messages several people accepted Jesus as their Lord and Savior and many others relationship with the Lord grew stronger. I have many times received feedback from friends like "That message was meant directly for me" or they would ask me "How did you know what I was going through?" My response has always been, "I didn't know, but God did." Three years ago I started posting the daily message on face-book and twitter, and this ministry absolutely exploded. We are reaching over 2000 people every day, all over the World. There were a few people on face-book who urged me to write a book about the messages. One person specifically kept pressing the issue, Annamarie Longfellow. Thank you so much Annamarie.

Many have asked where I get the messages from. I know they are definitely Heaven sent. As far as I know they are all 100 percent original. They come in different ways, mostly during a little quiet time with the Lord, other times it may be a song verse, a personal experience or there are times when I feel led to ask someone what the message of the day is. However I receive them, I know that they are meant for someone who is receiving them. I do not feel that I am special in any way or have a special hot line to God, but I do thank the Lord every day for using me as a vessel for His message. One thing we must all know and remember is that God still speaks today we just have to make sure we are listening.

Now you can read the book any way you choose, but I did write it more as a daily devotional. I send one new message everyday so it really did make sense. The stories are kept short so as to make it easy to read any time you get a spare moment. I tried to keep the messages in the order that I received them, except the first one, after who am I to mess with God's order of things. I included an area to write your thoughts and feelings about the message and how it may apply to your life.

I hope and pray that you enjoy this book and it helps in your continuing daily walk with Jesus. I promise that as long as God keeps whispering to me, I will continue to share with anyone who wants to listen.

God bless,
Jeff Odell

Chapter 1

You can always face the world head on because Jesus has your back.

I START WITH THIS WHISPER because it is my favorite. It makes me feel empowered when doubt, nerves, and fear creep up and try to stop me from doing what the Lord has called me to do. I pray that this will also help you on your journey with Jesus.

As Christians, we should have a quiet confidence knowing that as we face each new day in this world and all its challenges, if we keep the Spirit of Jesus in our hearts, He will never forsake us. When we feel attacked on all sides, know that Jesus is always here to cover and protect us, just as a good shepherd protects his flock from hungry wolves. We can be assured that the world will send wolves our way, but know it doesn't matter. Even if an entire pack comes our way, with our faith in Jesus, and his promises to us, we will overcome.

We all can be empowered knowing that with Jesus' Holy Spirit, we can accomplish many great and wonderful things in His Holy name. We can stand tall and proclaim the good news of Christ without fear. We can pray in public, pray for healing and pray for tremendous miracles and be assured that all prayers will be answered.

Know that anywhere we go today and any challenge we face, we can go with peace and confidence knowing that Jesus has our backs. God bless.

VERSE: **1 Peter 1:5 (NLT)** *"And through your faith, God is protecting you by his power until you receive this salvation, which is ready to be revealed on the last day for all to see."*

Thoughts and Feelings:

_____

_____

_____

_____

_____

_____

_____

_____

_____

_____

DATE: _____

Chapter 2

The true showing of God's love is not in the wonderful miracles that He performs, but it is in the everyday patience and love He has for us.

W<small>E ALL CAN AGREE</small> that God's miracles are wonderful, whether the miracle is a much needed physical healing or God interceding in a major event in our lives. These acts of God are tremendously powerful and life changing in our times of dire circumstances. Thankfully, we do not need these huge miracles every day.

What we all do need daily is God's love, patience, and understanding as we often stumble our way through life. Our lives are full of temptations and challenges, and while most of the time we make the wise choices, sometimes we make bad decisions. At these times, we allow temptation to grab hold of our sinful nature and either consciously or subconsciously we commit a sin. After, these times of indiscretion, guilt and repenting follow. This is when we must thank the Lord for the miracle of His endless mercy and love that He shows us.

I pray that as we go throughout our day, we don't try the Lords patience, but when we do, give thanks to the Lord for His eternal grace and love.

VERSE: **Lamentations 3:22 (NLT)** *"The faithful love of the Lord never ends! His mercies never cease."*

Thoughts and Feelings:

_____

_____

_____

_____

_____

_____

_____

_____

_____

_____

DATE _____

Chapter 3

When we are lost, we must use our G.P.S.: God's Prayer Service. He always shows us the way.

W E ALL FEEL LOST in life at times, not knowing which way to turn or even how we got to where we are. Often we are lost because we have tried to lead ourselves. It could be that we may have been forgetting to read the "Road Map of Life," God's Holy Bible, so we strayed off the right path. Perhaps we just joined in with the crowd, thinking maybe they knew where they were going, only to be like a lemming and follow until we fall off a cliff. Maybe we thought we were being led by a good shepherd that turned out to be a big bad wolf. Whatever the reason, we sometimes get off course.

Especially in these times, we must know that God is only a prayer away. Our God wants, expects, and desires for us to cry out for Him in our time of need. God does not want any of us to go through life with bad or no direction. He so much wants His lost ones to find their way. Even though we may have made a few wrong turns in life and traveled down roads that we had no business being on, God does not want us lost.

The world will give us all sorts of road blocks, crazy signs, and detours, but know that if we allow ourselves to be led by God we will all make it home safe and sound.

VERSE: **Psalm 32: 8 (NLT)** *"The Lord says,*
I will guide you along the best pathway for your
life. I will advise you and watch over you."

Thoughts and feelings:

_____

_____

_____

_____

_____

_____

_____

_____

_____

_____

_____

_____

_____

DATE _____ _____

Photo by William Lee

Chapter 4

Material things are nice but the real blessings come in the people that God places in our lives.

HOW MANY TIMES HAVE we heard or maybe said to ourselves, "I am blessed with a beautiful home," or "I am blessed with a fine car"? A home that is not filled with family or a car driven to visit nobody, is really no blessing at all. The finest, most expensive meal will taste bitter if eaten alone and not spiced with good conversation with someone we love. Traveling and seeing the great wonders of the world means nothing if we travel alone.

It is our loved ones that fill our homes and it is the friends and family that we drive to see that are real blessings in life. The laughter and sharing of the bountiful harvest with friends is what makes a meal wonderful. Any road we travel will be filled with all sorts of wonders to see if we share the adventure with someone else. We can find a blessing in our family members, lifelong friends, acquaintances, or someone passing on the street that offers a smile.

Let us never hesitate to take a moment and thank the Lord our God for the wonderful people that He places in our lives to make our journey a lot less lonely and so much more blessed.

> *VERSE*: **1 John 4:11-12 (NLT)** *"Dear friends, since God loved us that much, we surely ought to love each other. No one has ever seen God. But if we love each other, God lives in us, and his love is brought to full expression in us."*

Thoughts and Feelings

_____

_____

_____

_____

_____

_____

_____

_____

_____

DATE _____

Chapter 5

Sink our roots deep in our faith, nourish ourselves daily in God's word, and grow closer to the Son, Jesus Christ.

L IKE TREES OF A forest that sink their roots deep and strong, we also must be planted firmly in our faith in Jesus Christ our Lord. Always standing strong, not allowing the storms of life to uproot us. In our lives, we are swayed in one direction or another, but it is our faith that always will return us straight toward the Son.

As Christians we must continue to grow in our faith by reading and feeding daily on God's Holy Bible. This will nourish our faith, allowing us to continually grow closer to the Lord each day. Having God's Holy Word flowing in us will strengthen us when the storms of life come blowing through. The more God's word becomes a part of us, the more others will see and be blessed by the fruits of the Spirit we will bear.

As we grow in our faith and knowledge, we must also grow closer in our personal relationship with Jesus Christ. Turn our faces to Heaven and bask in the light and love from Jesus Christ. For it is in Him that we find joy, comfort, peace, love, and happiness, for Jesus is the best friend we all have.

My prayer is that we all grow deeper in our faith, stronger in God's Holy word, and closer in our relationship with the Son, Jesus Christ.

> *VERSE*: **Ephesians 3:17-18 (NLT)** *"Then Christ will make his home in your hearts as you trust in him. Your roots will grow down into God's love and keep you strong. And may you have the power to understand, as all God's people should, how wide, how long, how high, and how deep his love is."*

Thoughts and feelings

DATE _____

Chapter 6

Open our hearts completely and be filled with a most wonderful Love, Joy, and Peace that only can come from our Lord Jesus Christ.

THIS MESSAGE IS VERY special to me. The Lord has had me deliver it in many of the sermons I have preached. The Lord also led me to call my ministry "Open Heart Ministry." God's desire is to bless us and fill us with His Holy Spirit until we are absolutely overflowing with His love. But unless we open ourselves completely to God, we are limiting ourselves in receiving all that the Lord has for us. Be assured that the Lord wants to bless us with all the wonders of Heaven, for we are His children who He loves completely and He will never forsake us.

When we open ourselves completely to Jesus, we open ourselves to be filled with His Holy Spirit. We will be filled with the most wonderful love that we cannot help but share with others. We receive exciting, exhilarating, and powerful joy that will be all but impossible to contain. The peace we will feel will remove all worries and stresses knowing that we are led and protected by the Great Shepherd Jesus Christ.

The Lord our God wants to bless us completely and abundantly to where His love flows out of us which in turn blesses others. Let us remove all fear and open our hearts completely to all and everything that the Lord our God has for us.

> *Verse*: **Ephesians 6:23-24 (NLT)** *"Peace be with you, dear brothers and sisters, and may God the Father and the Lord Jesus Christ give you love with faithfulness. May God's grace be eternally upon all who love our Lord Jesus Christ."*

Thoughts and Feeling:

_____

_____

_____

_____

_____

_____

_____

_____

_____

DATE _____

Chapter 7

Whatever pain or problem we have, Jesus will see us through.

Pain and problems, whatever they may be, are part of life. As Christians we are not immune to them, but thankfully as Christians, we do not go through them alone. We go through them with the Great Comforter Jesus Christ.

While there is much pain and suffering that the Lord keeps us from, sometimes we have to face problems. There are lessons we must learn from these problems. We may learn a lesson in patience, faith, hope, or the importance of leaning on God. Know that as we walk with Jesus, we do not face these problems alone and a blessed lesson will be learned. I myself have been dealing with a back problem for three years now. It is going through this problem that I have leaned on God and held fast, knowing that there is a blessing behind this time of suffering. It is this problem that made this book possible. God has a reason, a plan, and a purpose behind all the things that happen in our lives.

Let us always be of good cheer. For whatever pain or problem we are carrying with us today, know that we do not bear the load alone.

VERSE: **Hebrews 4:16 (NLT)** *"So let us come boldly to the throne of our gracious God. There we will receive his mercy, and we will find grace to help us when we need it most."*

Thoughts and feeling

_____

_____

_____

_____

_____

_____

_____

_____

_____

_____

_____

*DATE*_____

Chapter 8

We often get impatient waiting on God to answer our prayers, but keep in mind how often the Lord has to wait for us to answer His call.

G OD BEGINS ANSWERING PRAYERS the moment we pray or even before. Some of His answers are felt immediately while some we do not see the answers until a much later time, yet know God is always working on our behalf. Our Lord knows our needs and our desires and hears all our prayers. God also knows when His answer to our prayers will be of the biggest blessing.

Knowing that God hears and answers all our prayers, one question must be asked of us. How many times have we felt that God led us to do something, but we have made Him wait or just ignored His call completely? Maybe He led us to show someone charity, kindness, or love? But we waited until it would be more convenient for us or just didn't do it at all. Perhaps we were led to tell a stranger that Jesus loves him or her, but out of fear, just ignored giving the stranger the message. How many of us have felt led to volunteer for a church committee or teach a Sunday school class but later talked ourselves out of it? If this sounds familiar, welcome to the crowd, brothers and sisters.

A few years ago, I was working around a person I had never met. Suddenly, I felt an overwhelming feeling to tell him "Jesus says, yes." For hours I tried to get up enough nerve and looked for the right moment to share this message with him. I never did. I felt tremendously horrible. That night I prayed and promised God that I would never again ignore Him when He calls on me to do something. A couple months later, He gave me another opportunity, and you can trust me that I did not even hesitate for a minute to deliver His message. When I gave this person the message, tears began filling her eyes and she knew exactly what I was talking about. In these Heaven sent whispers, there have been some messages that I thought were odd, but I obediently sent them anyway. After I send these messages, I will get a response from someone or a few people on how the message spoke to them and how it applied to their life. These responses leave my eyes filled up with tears out of shear humbleness and appreciation to the Lord for using me. We don't always know why God asks us to do something but we can be assured that someone will be blessed by it.

Let us always try to be patient when waiting for God's answers to our prayers. Let us never hesitate to act on what the Good Lord is telling us to do. Ultimately, when we feel like we are growing impatient waiting on God's answers to our prayers, let us be mindful of all the loving patience that He has shown while waiting on us.

VERSE: **Colossians 3: 12 (NLT)** *"Since God chose you to be the Holy people he loves, you must clothe yourselves with tenderhearted mercy, kindness, humility, gentleness, and patience."*

Thoughts and Feeling:

_____

_____

_____

_____

_____

_____

_____

_____

_____

_____

_____

_____

_____

_____

*DATE*_____

Photo by William Lee

Chapter 9

Have our Hearts Burn with Passion for Christ, then things that anger us and make our blood boil won't seem quite as hot.

I THINK IT WOULD BE safe to say that almost every Christian in the free world has seen the movie "The Passion of the Christ." The movie brought many of us to tears and to a new understanding of how passionately Jesus loves us. The savage beating, the cruelty, and disrespect shown to Jesus depicted on the screen was hard to watch. Jesus went through all that because He deeply loves each and every one of us.

Our hearts should burn just as passionately for Jesus. We must desire to be always in his will, love, and peace. It is being in Jesus' Spirit that we are able to deal with all the world angers us with. When in His will, we can look past the inconsiderate acts of others. When filled with Jesus' passionate love, we can smile with joy in our hearts when we are treated with contempt. When filled with His peace we can be calm through all the storms of life.

Let us all be filled with the Spirit of Christ, so all the things that would otherwise make us furious will somehow not seem that important to require such a hot-headed reaction.

> *VERSE*: **Ephesians 4: 24-27 (NLT)** *"Put on your new nature, created to be like God—truly righteous and holy. So stop telling lies. Let us tell our neighbors the truth, for we are all parts of the same body. And "don't sin by letting anger control you don't let the sun go down while you are still angry, for anger gives a foothold to the devil."*

Thoughts and Feelings:

_____

_____

_____

_____

_____

_____

_____

_____

_____

_____

DATE: _____

Chapter 10

God will not promise you the world for having faith in Him, but He will guarantee you Heaven.

HAVING FAITH IN GOD does not mean that as Christians we will drive the nicest cars or live in the nicest houses or have the biggest bank accounts. All of that would be nice and if God sees fit to give that to us, He will. But in the end, the world's stuff is the world's stuff and when we pass away we leave it all behind.

The Bible tells us that if we believe in Jesus Christ as our Lord and Savior, we will spend eternity with Him in paradise. There is a feeling of peacefulness in this promise. This guarantee gives us strength to persevere when times are tough. When we try to think of what Heaven will be like, many pictures run through our minds just imagining its beauty. There is nothing on earth that could ever match the joy we will feel when we step through the gates of Heaven. The song "I Can Only Imagine," by Bart Millard and Mercy Me, comes to mind when I think of the first moments we will spend in Heaven with Jesus Christ our Lord.

Most people would not be willing to share their mansions or Ferrari sports cars with us. Yet, as Christians, one of the greatest joys we will ever feel is when we share Jesus and the promise of an eternity in Heaven with others. The things of this world in no way will ever equal all the treasures we have stored away in Heaven.

VERSE: **Matthew 6: 20-21 (NLT)** *"Store your treasures in heaven, where moths and rust cannot destroy, and thieves do not break in and steal. Wherever your treasure is, there the desires of your heart will also be."*

Thoughts and feelings

_____

_____

_____

_____

_____

_____

_____

_____

_____

_____

*DATE*_____

Chapter 11

I like the spike, the high five, and the chest
bump, a dunk over the cross bar-- man, can
they jump-- but my very favorite has to be
when athletes give glory to God by pointing
to Heaven or simply taking a knee.

AN ATHLETE MAKES A great play and he does a dance, another makes a touchdown and jumps into the stands, while others high five, low five, front bump and back bump each other. All this in celebration at what they have done. All this to say, "Look at me, see how great and talented I am." But there are those that simply and quietly point to Heaven and say, "Thank You, God," or they take a knee in the corner of the end zone and offer a prayer of thanks to God. This inspires me that these men, that some people hold larger than life, can be humble with thousands of screaming fans singing their praises. One thing I would like to see is an athlete drop an important pass and still point up and say, "Thank You, God, for just allowing me to try."

In our daily lives and accomplishments, do we thank the Lord our God? When we get a pat on the back from the boss, do we give the glory and credit to God who gave us our abilities? When we finish a task at work, do we take a knee in a prayer of thankfulness? Do we give thanks to God that we are alive and are able to work and provide for our families?

Though we may not be a household name or make millions of dollars or parade across a televisions screen, let us still be thankful for the talents the Lord has blessed us with. As we go throughout our days, let us often take a minute to thank God for all the talents He has given us and all the blessings to come.

VERSE: **Colossians 3:17 (NLT)** *"And whatever you do or say, do it as a representative of the Lord Jesus, giving thanks through him to God the Father."*

Thoughts and Feelings:

_____

_____

_____

_____

_____

_____

_____

_____

*DATE*_____

Chapter 12

BELIEVE whatever you want, but KNOW that Jesus Christ is your Lord and Savior.

BELIEFS ARE LIKE OPINIONS, we all have thousands of them, and no one person is completely alike. Another truth is that people love to share them, even when no one really wants to hear them. The world will give all sorts of opinions of what or who they believe God to be. They have no Bible, no doctrine, and no proof, all they have is just an opinion of God. The differing of beliefs is not just a world issue, but it is also within the Christian community.

Christians cannot even agree on some fundamental beliefs. What is the right way for a person to be baptized, should it be by submersion or just sprinkling on the Holy water? Should women cut their hair or let it grow? Should confessing a sin be done to a priest or simply going in repentance to God ourselves? These are just a few of the beliefs that Christians disagree on. What is right, wrong, or pretty close is insignificant as long as we KNOW with all our heart, mind, and soul that Jesus Christ is our Lord and personal Savior. John 3:16 tells us to "Believe" to have eternal life. My prayer is that we can all confidently say that we know with the very essence of our soul that Jesus Christ is our king, redeemer, Lord, and Savior. As we go on through the years, the differing opinions of how to worship Jesus will just have to be that, different opinions. But take heart, my brothers and sisters, and know that Jesus will lead us in the right direction. Jesus would not and will not forsake one of His own who has a heartfelt love and belief in Him.

What it all comes down to is that when we are asked what we believe, the best answer we can respond with is "I don't believe in, but I know in Jesus Christ!"

VERSE: **2 Peter 3: 17-18 (NLT)** *"I am warning you ahead of time, dear friends. Be on guard so that you will not be carried away by the errors of these wicked people and lose your own secure footing. Rather, you must grow in the grace and knowledge of our Lord and Savior Jesus Christ. All glory to him, both now and forever! Amen."*

Thoughts and Feelings:

_____

_____

_____

_____

_____

_____

_____

_____

*DATE:*_____

Chapter 13

Enjoy the journey of life; God will provide all you need for the trip.

WHAT A WONDERFUL GIFT is this life that the Lord has blessed us with. What an awesome journey God has placed us on. What a joy it is to never really know what is around the next corner. But think how at peace we could be if we would stop worrying about the little things, like are we there yet and do we have enough to complete our journey. How blessed would we be if we had enough Faith to know that God will provide all our needs.

Journeys are supposed to be joyful, exciting, and enlightening. Oh boy, do we mess that up sometimes. We worry about each and every little thing. We worry, what if this or that happens, do we have enough money to last, what about the next meal? Then we scream, "I'm scared!" My wife and I go through this sometimes. But then the Lord reminds us that, thankfully, we have never been a day without a meal or a place to lay our heads. Of course, there are times in our lives when the pickings are slim, but know that through it all, the Lord provides everything for our wonderful journey through life.

We are God's special children and God, as our father, will bless us with all we ever need. So let's get off the worry couch and start walking down the wonderful, exciting, joy-filled path that is life.

VERSE: **Luke 12: 22-23 (NLT)** *"Then, turning to his disciples, Jesus said, "That is why I tell you not to worry about everyday life—whether you have enough food to eat or enough clothes to wear. For life is more than food and your body more than clothing."*

Thoughts and feelings:

_____

_____

_____

_____

_____

_____

_____

_____

_____

_____

_____

_____

_____

_____

_____

*DATE*_____

Photo by William Lee

Chapter 14

If what we say and do pleases people but dishonors God, we have gained nothing, but if what we say and do honors God, we gained his kingdom.

HAVE WE EVER TOLD an inappropriate joke or made a snide comment to get a laugh? Have we ever bullied or picked on someone to gain acceptance from the crowd? Have we ever joined in some worldly thing just to fit in? I am sure we have at some point in our lives felt the peer pressure and have allowed ourselves to fall into these situations. There is no good excuse for it, but this does happen.

Being a Christian at times is not easy, especially when the people that are around us are not Christians. Our fear of being made fun of or ridiculed for our beliefs is all too real at times. It is in these times that we must stand strong in our faith in Jesus and resist the temptation to sin just to fit in. It would be much better to be counted in Jesus' crowd than any group that the world has to offer.

Let us be sure never to find ourselves judging others for their actions, for this is not of our concern. Let us find ourselves standing strong in our faith and in the goodness of Jesus Christ our Lord.

VERSE: **Matthew 5:10 (NLT)** *"My prayer is that when we are in these tough situations that we will find the strength, comfort and peace in the Lord to stand for and do what is right."*

Thoughts and feelings:

_____

_____

_____

_____

_____

_____

_____

_____

_____

_____

_____

DATE: _____

Chapter 15

When waiting on an answer, a blessing or deliverance, be patient; God is always right on time.

URING MY OVER THREE-YEAR ordeal with two bad discs and back surgery, how often have I prayed for deliverance from the horrible pain? My faith in knowing that there has got to be a tremendous blessing behind this time of suffering surely has helped me through. Knowing that God's answer is coming allows me to keep going from day to day. Though it may not be a back injury or even a physical problem at all, each one of us has our own dilemmas that we need deliverance from.

We all may have faith in knowing that God will give us our answers, blessings, and deliverance, but the patience department is where we sometimes fall short. Patience is definitely a virtue, but it is a virtue we need to work on. Know that God hears our cries and our prayers; He knows our needs and when they are needed most.

So let us wait patiently and faithfully for God's wonderful answers, blessing, and deliverance, for they are assuredly on their way.

VERSE: **James 5:11 (NLT)** *"We give great honor to those who endure under suffering. For instance, you know about Job, a man of great endurance. You can see how the Lord was kind to him at the end, for the Lord is full of tenderness and mercy."*

Thoughts and feelings:

_____

_____

_____

_____

_____

_____

_____

_____

_____

_____

_____

_____

DATE: _____

Chapter 16

Live for God and put all our faith in God. Then even in the darkest hour we can proclaim that God is good and we will be victorious.

T O LIVE FOR GOD is to do whatever we can do to bring honor, respect, and glory to God. To live for God is to lead others to God's grace. To live for God is for the Lord to be the very essence of what we stand for, look to, and trust in.

To put all our faith in the Lord is to trust that He will supply all our needs. Have faith knowing that the Lord will give us strength when we are weak and will comfort us in times of trouble and sorrow. Have eternal peace in the Lord's promise of grace.

Just as Job had tragedies and troubles in his life, we too will face our own dark hours. Like Job who stayed strong in his faith, we also must never waiver in ours, knowing that the Lord's loving light will again one day shine on us.

When we are living for and have all our faith in God, we can strongly stand tall and call on the Lord to drive away the darkness and envelop us with his light so that we can claim victory in His Holy Name. Arise, my brothers and sisters, for the Lord's victory over our problems is at hand.

VERSE: **1 John 5 1-5 (NLT)** *"Everyone who believes that Jesus is the Christ has become a child of God. And everyone who loves the Father loves his children, too. We know we love God's children if we love God and obey his commandments. Loving God means keeping his commandments, and his commandments are not burdensome. For every child of God defeats this evil world and we achieve this victory through our faith. And who can win this battle against the world? Only those who believe that Jesus is the Son of God."*

Thoughts and feelings:

_____

_____

_____

_____

_____

_____

_____

_____

_____

_____

DATE _____

Chapter 17

Before our problems induce anger, envy, hate, doom, fear, dread and despair, give them to God and induce joy, peace and trust in the Lord.

PROBLEMS ARE PART OF life and they can make us go through a wide variety of emotions, with most of them being very negative. These negative emotions do not solve any problems; they actually make us feel worse. Unfortunately, being a Christian, we too must face some gut-wrenching problems. The difference is how, as Christians, we are to handle them.

What if we didn't have to let our problems get the best of us? What if we could just give our problems to someone else and let that person solve them for us? As Christians, we can give them to God; in fact, He wants us to. God wants us to lean on His love that He has for us. God wants us to put all our trust in Him. God wants to fill us full of His peace and joy in knowing that He is our Lord, our Savior, our Comforter, our One and only.

Life gives us problems, but God gives us solutions. So, let us lay our problems and worries at the feet of the Lord and get on living with pure happiness in this wonderful life that the Lord has given us.

VERSE: **Philippians 4: 6** *"Don't worry about anything; instead, pray about everything. Tell God what you need, and thank him for all he has done. Then you will experience God's peace, which exceeds anything we can understand. His peace will guard your hearts and minds as you live in Christ Jesus."*

Thoughts and feelings:

_____

_____

_____

_____

_____

_____

_____

_____

_____

_____

_____

DATE _____

Chapter 18

Be not overly confident in ourselves, but be humbly confident that the Lord gives us strength to accomplish anything.

NOT BEING HUMBLE WILL sometimes make us stumble. Some may call it karma, but when someone who is smug and egotistical gets brought back down to earth, there seems to be a sense of justice. Not for them, but for the rest of us.

The Lord has blessed each of us with our own special talents. Using these talents is what God expects of us. But let us remember to give the glory to God for what we accomplish with them. Our confidence should not be in ourselves but in the strength and goodness of the Lord our God.

With the strength of the Lord, any and every thing that we call on God to do, can and will be accomplished through our faith in Him. The Bible tells us that we can move mountains through our faith in God. A true story I once heard on the radio brings this to light. A 16-year-old boy was riding with his mother in his home town. They passed a small mountain that had been there since the town was founded. The boy turned to his mother and told her that he was going to build a church on the spot where the mountain was. She told him he couldn't build a church on that spot because the mountain was there. He calmly told her that God will move it. She smiled with joy at her son's faith but did not believe at all that her son's plans would come through. A couple of years later, a wealthy man bought the mountain. The man had plans to build a shopping center on that spot. The man brought in bulldozers and dump trucks and before long, the mountain was gone. Now the wealthy man was ready to build the shopping center, but things fell through and he was unable to build it. With the land being of no use to him anymore, he placed it for sale and the mother's son was able to buy it and build a church on that spot.

The young man supplied no strength in moving the mountain except for the tremendous strength of his faith. What he proclaimed in the Lord's name happened in the Lord's name. Let our confidence be in our faith in God; and for all that we accomplish in our lives, let us always give the glory to God, who makes it possible.

*VERSE: **2 Corinthians 3: 4-5 (NLT)*** *"We are confident of all this because of our great trust in God through Christ. It is not that we think we are qualified to do anything on our own. Our qualification comes from God."*

Thoughts and Feelings:

_____

_____

_____

_____

_____

_____

*DATE*_____

Chapter 19

God's blessings can be found in our blood, sweat and tears that we shed while working to accomplish something to help our fellow man.

THERE IS NO GREATER feeling than to know that we have changed a person's life for the better. To see the smile on their face, to hear the gratitude in their voice, and to be engulfed in the joy of their hug for what we have done for them is one of the greatest blessing we can ever feel.

I live in South Mississippi and was here when Hurricane Katrina came through and tore down and wiped out people homes completely. I have a very dear friend, Sister Lillian Gray, who lost everything. When she returned home after the storm there was no home to return to. Her house and all her belongings were completely gone. Her home, where all her mementos of her 80-plus years were stored, was gone. All her pictures, including pictures of her three boys who went missing years earlier while they were out shrimping in the gulf, were washed away. Gone was a cherished Bible of her Mother who had passed. Though this was devastating to her, it was the strength of her faith that pulled her through. Her son Pete and his family, who lived next door, lost everything also. For the first month after the storm, Sister Lillian and her family stayed at the church and slept on blow-up mattresses. Then they moved into FEMA trailers, and next Sister Lillian and Pete and his family moved into a single-wide trailer they bought, but it still didn't quite feel like home. Two years after the storm, she was contacted by a church that organized volunteers to come and rebuild houses for people. For the next few months, volunteer after volunteer came from all over the country and worked on a house for Sister Lillian and a house for Pete, his wife Patty and their two daughters Sarah and Amanda. The charity that these workers showed was inspiring. Excitement and joy could be seen in the family's eyes as they watched their new homes being constructed. Finally, as the last coat of paint was drying, the keys to the two new houses were handed to Pete and his family and to Sister Lillian. These volunteers didn't just build two houses; they built two homes filled with the charitable goodness of Jesus Christ our Lord. The true gratitude that this family felt is far too great to measure.

When we have the opportunity to give of ourselves for the good of others, let us not ask for or expect anything in return. Let us not think how hard it was to do, how much it cost or how long it took. Just knowing that with the spirit of Jesus Christ in our hearts we did something good, and that is where the blessing lies, just between God and us.

VERSE: **Isaiah 58:7-8 (NLT)** *"Share your food with the hungry, and give shelter to the homeless. Give clothes to those who need them, and do not hide from relatives who need your help. Then your salvation will come like the dawn, and your wounds will quickly heal. Your godliness will lead you forward, and the glory of the Lord will protect you from behind."*

Thoughts and feelings:

_____

_____

_____

_____

_____

_____

_____

_____

_____

_____

_____

_____

_____

_____

*DATE*_____

Sister Lillian Gray

Chapter 20

God's plan for us was set in place long before we were born. So out of love and respect for God, let us try not to mess it up too badly.

ONE TRUTH IS THAT God has a plan for each and every one of us and has had one long before we were born. This can be very humbling to realize, but then it can be very powerful too. What an awesome thing to know that we have a purpose in God's Holy Kingdom and that God is depending on us. What an honor to do the Lord's work, how strengthened we feel when we are doing something to further God's Holy Kingdom. What a feeling of joy to know that our efforts count to God.

Nothing can stand in our way when we are fulfilling God's wonderful plan for us. Well maybe one thing; us. Yes, we are the only thing that knocks God's perfect plan for us off its perfect path. We all have our little quirks, our insecurities, our sinful nature, and our just plain bad ideas. How many times have we watched somebody do something and fumble around until you just want to tell them to "get out of the way, I will do it myself"? I wonder if God ever feels that way.

God has a perfect plan for each one of us and has had one long before we were born. Let us always look to God for His guidance, make sure that we stay in His will, and let nothing stand in our way when we are working for the Lord.

> *Verse:* **Jeremiah 1:5 (NLT)** *"I knew before I formed you in your mother's womb. Before you were born I set you apart and appointed you as my prophet to the nations."*

Thoughts and Feelings:

_____

_____

_____

_____

_____

_____

_____

_____

_____

_____

DATE: _____

Chapter 21

Evidence of us getting stronger in the Lord can be seen when our desire to please God exceeds our temptation to commit sin.

TEMPTATION IS A POWERFUL weapon of the Devil. Unfortunately he knows our weaknesses and will use them against us any and every chance he can. But if we stand strong and resist the temptation to sin because of our heartfelt desire to please God, then we have gained honor in the eyes of the Lord.

One truth we must understand is that the closer we get to God, the more the devil will try to attack us. Satan does not want us to preach God's word, share the gift of grace, and fulfill God's purpose for us. The devil wants to tempt us with our weaknesses, fill our minds full of doubt, and ultimately separate us from God.

In these times when Satan comes against us, let us stand strong in our faith. Let us realize that mere moments of worldly pleasure do not outweigh--in any way, shape or form-- an eternity of peace, joy and love in Heaven with Jesus Christ. In our times of weakness, call upon the Lord, and He will strengthen us so that we can stay in his perfect will.

We must stand strong my brothers and sisters. Know that while we are under attack by temptation, we can instead choose to follow our desire to help others and please God.

Verse: James 4:7(NLT)   *"…resist the devil and he will flee from you"*

Thoughts and Feelings:

_____

_____

_____

_____

_____

_____

_____

_____

_____

_____

*DATE:*_____

Chapter 22

Relax, take a deep breath and smile. Allow God to take control.

A FEW YEARS AGO, I was coaching a softball game and we were winning by quite a few runs. The other team's pitcher was named Courtney, and she was struggling to throw strikes. I was in the coaching box and I heard the first baseman yell to her pitcher in the sweetest little southern girl voice, "Relax, Courtney. Take a deep breath and smile." My team scored a couple more runs and we won the game easily, but that little statement of encouragement has stuck with me for years.

This past year God reminded me of this sweet encouragement. My oldest daughter, Samantha, was in an uproar about one thing or another, asking what she should do, where she should turn. While she was on her rant, I felt God speak, tell her to "relax, take a deep breath and smile and allow God to take control." This stopped her in her tracks and she smiled and understood. Everything worked out fine for her, not because of all her worrying, but because of her faith in God.

We all have our moments when it feels like our life is out of control, when we can't get anything right, when we don't know what the right answers are to our dilemmas. It is these moments that relaxing, taking a breath, smiling and allowing God to take control is the very best answer.

> *VERSE:* **Romans 15: 5-6 (NLT)** *"May God, who gives this patience and encouragement, help you live in complete harmony with each other, as is fitting for followers of Christ Jesus. Then all of you can join together with one voice, giving praise and glory to God, the Father of our Lord Jesus Christ."*

Thoughts and Feelings:

_____

_____

_____

_____

_____

_____

_____

_____

_____

_____

_____

*DATE*_____

Chapter 23

Do not just believe in Jesus, but know in Jesus! Then powerfully pray and accomplish wonderful things in the name of the Lord.

To know in Jesus is to never doubt, never sway, no matter what Satan throws our way. Knowing in Jesus solidifies our testimony, adds boldness to our witnessing, and empowers our prayers. Knowing in Christ means that He is the very core of our mind, heart, and soul.

When we know in Jesus, then our testimony becomes more than a story we tell; it becomes a truth that we proclaim. When we know in Christ, our Christian walk becomes more honest, more powerful, and more evident of the Lord in our daily lives. When we know in our Lord, witnessing becomes a passion to share the love and grace of the Lord with everyone we meet. When we know in Jesus, we are empowered to be able to withstand all challenges that the world hurls at us, not hoping we will overcome but knowing that victory will be ours in the name of the Lord. When we know in God, we can confidently pray, knowing that our requests are in God's hands and they will be answered. Knowing in Jesus

Christ as our Lord and Savior means that in His name we will accomplish many wonderful and amazing things.

Whether we say "we believe" or "we know" does not really matter as long as in our hearts and soul we know completely that Jesus Christ is out Lord and Savior.

VERSE: **Jude 1: 24-25** *"Now all glory to God, who is able to keep you from falling away and will bring you with great joy into his glorious presence without a single fault. All glory to him who alone is God, our Savior through Jesus Christ our Lord. All glory, majesty, power, and authority are his before all time, and in the present, and beyond all time! Amen."*

Thoughts and feelings:

_____

_____

_____

_____

_____

_____

_____

_____

_____

DATE: _____

Chapter 24

Instead of wasting our time counting our problems, take time to count our blessings and rejoice in the Lord and all His greatness.

MY BACK HURTS ALL the time, I cannot do even the simplest of tasks without pain and suffering, but I am blessed. I know that the pain will one day ease. I am blessed with a wonderful family that helps me and loves me, and I know that the Lord has a blessing behind this time of struggle.

Money problems, health problems, job problems, family problems, relationship problems, or any other problem we face in life, will at times seem to take over our every waking thought. I can positively say that not any problem has ever been solved by endless hours of worry. All worrying does is give us gray hair, wrinkles, ulcers, heart attacks, and strokes. Let us always know that the problems we give to God are no longer for us to worry about. We far too often place our problems on the Lord's altar only to pick them back up and take them home with us and worry about them some more.

A far better use of our time is counting our blessings. Think how blessed we are with families and friends that love us. Think about how God supplies us with everything we need from day to day. Count how blessed we are with God's great gifts of life, love, and grace. These are the thoughts that should occupy our minds constantly. Counting our blessings will lead to smiles, laughter, joy, peace, and lots of God's love to share with others.

A problem worried about is still a problem tomorrow but a blessing counted will grow into a blessing we can share with others for years to come.

> *VERSE:* **Philippians 4: 4-7 (NLT)** *"Always be full of joy in the Lord. I say it again—rejoice! Let everyone see that you are considerate in all you do. Remember, the Lord is coming soon.*
>
> *Don't worry about anything; instead, pray about everything. Tell God what you need, and thank him for all he has done. Then you will experience God's peace, which exceeds anything we can understand. His peace will guard your hearts and minds as you live in Christ Jesus."*

Thoughts and Feelings:

_____

_____

_____

_____

_____

_____

DATE _____

Chapter 25

Do not measure ourselves on being better than wicked men, but strive to measure up to the goodness of God.

HERE'S AN OLD JOKE: Two guys are being chased by a bear. One man stops to put on his sneakers. The other guy says, "you can't out run that bear." The guy in the sneakers runs past his buddy, telling him, "I don't have to be faster than the bear. I just have to be faster than you!"

We must remember that a sin is a sin; not any one outweighs another. So if we have never killed anyone but we have told a lie, we are no better than a mass murderer in God's eyes. Furthermore, if the murderer truly finds Jesus and becomes one of His children, then he will enter the gates of Heaven while the liar that never repents and accepts Jesus will be left on the outside looking in. In a way this may not seem fair. The Bible is clear on this, that the only way to Heaven is through repenting our sins and accepting Jesus Christ as our Lord and Savior. As Christians, our goal, our role model, our standard must be to live a life as perfect as Jesus Christ. We can never reach this completely but as Christians we must do our best to try.

If we were to place two Christians in the joke at the beginning, the one with the shoes would offer them to his Christian brother or they would run in opposite directions, praying for and placing each other in God's hands. Either way we look at it, we should always strive to be as close to the goodness of God as we can and help others to get to know Jesus Christ.

VERSE: **Proverbs 2: 20-22 (NLT)** *"Follow the steps of good men instead, and stay on the paths of the righteous. For only the godly will live in the land, and those with integrity will remain in it. But the wicked will be removed from the land, and the treacherous will be uprooted."*

Thoughts and Feelings:

_____

_____

_____

_____

_____

_____

_____

_____

_____

_____

DATE: _____

Chapter 26

The best Insurance is the Assurance that God keeps his promises.

MANY INSURANCE COMPANIES OFFER a wide variety of life insurance policies, yet not one of them can offer an after life insurance policy like the Good Lord does.

Insurance companies offer financial peace of mind to our families so that after our passing, their money worries will be taken care of. But insurance policies can be canceled and our loved ones will be left up to the government to take care of. My father-in-law for years would tell how he has a million dollars in life insurance policies for when he passes away. Unexpectedly, he began to suffer from diabetes and other physical problems, which forced him to retire early, so most of the life insurance policies, which added up to a million dollars, were canceled. After his passing, there was enough for the funeral, with only a little left. My mother-in-law now lives month to month on social security and has to cut corners anywhere she can; so much for the financial peace of mind.

As Christians, God gives us and our loved ones peace of mind and assurance, knowing that when we pass from this life, we will have an eternity with Him in Heaven. We can also feel assured that when our time comes, our loved ones who have passed will be standing at the Pearly Gates to welcome us in. God will not cancel His after life policy with us. He will not reduce it or tack on penalties. His after life policy, Grace, is written in stone and will be for eternity. My father-in-law's immediate family, including me, was in the room in his last moments. When he took his last breath, I know that I saw his spirit leave his body and ascend to Heaven. There was a peace that I felt knowing that this good man, Bob Evans, who loved the Lord and who his family loved, was in Heaven.

Let us always be thankful for God's grace that he gives us and his faithfulness in keeping his promises. We must take time to share God's assurance plan with everyone. Know that God keeps all his promises, both in life and after. Believe in Jesus Christ and be assured to spend an eternity with him in Heaven.

> *VERSE:* **Acts 2: 38-39 (NLT)** *"Peter replied, "Each of you must repent of your sins and turn to God, and be baptized in the name of Jesus Christ for the forgiveness of your sins. Then you will receive the gift of the Holy Spirit. This promise is to you, and to your children, and even to the Gentiles—all who have been called by the Lord our God."*

Thoughts and Feelings:

_____

_____

_____

_____

_____

_____

*DATE:*_____

Chapter 27

Trust in God and expect miracles.

TRUST IS DEFINED AS "reliance on the integrity, strength, ability, surety, etc., of a person or thing; confidence." How better could it be said? We rely on God's integrity that what he says in the Holy Bible is the truth. We rely on God's strength to carry us through the tough times in life. We rely on God's ability to help us, bless us, and provide all our daily needs. We rely on the surety we feel in God and his promises. Finally, it is the confidence in knowing that, in God, all is possible.

To trust in God is to know that he performs miracles. He gives us big miracles, little miracles, and daily miracles. The Bible is filled with accounts of some of the great miracles he has performed over the ages. Many of us can tell of miraculous things that the Lord has done in our lives. We can think of a time or two when little unexplained blessed events have happened in our lives. When we take time to think about it, we can realize and see that God's mighty hand was on the situation. Having our daily needs met, friendly smiles that brighten our day, making our last few dollars last until pay day, are just some of the wonderful miracles that let us know that God is with us daily, forever and always.

Miracles are unexplained events in which divine intervention is the most logical explanation. As Christians, we must always be mindful that God is the God of miracles and we can trust that he has some for us.

VERSE: **John 12: 44-46 (NLT)** *"Jesus shouted to the crowds, "If you trust me, you are trusting not only me, but also God who sent me. For when you see me, you are seeing the one who sent me. I have come as a light to shine in this dark world, so that all who put their trust in me will no longer remain in the dark."*

Thoughts and Feelings:

_____

_____

_____

_____

_____

_____

_____

_____

_____

_____

_____

_____

_____

_____

DATE: _____

Jeff Odell

Photo by William Lee

Chapter 28

a (B)eautiful, (L)oving (E)xpression and (S)weet (S)urprise (I)nitiated in the (N)ame of (G)od. (a BLESSING)

WHEN IT COMES TIME for me to send out the daily "Whisper from Heaven," I have at times felt led to ask those around me what is on their heart that day. This has always been a tremendous blessing, learning what is on the hearts of friends, family, and others. When I ask my wife, Melissa, what the message should be about today, she always gives me the same answer, "Blessings." I would like to think she says this because she feels so blessed to be married to me. Somehow, I do not think that is the reason she says it.

My wife and I often talk about how thankful we are to God for how blessed we are. As Christians we all are blessed in so many ways. We could almost in some ways, feel guilty for all we are blessed with, because there are those with less. We should understand that, while there are those who are less fortunate, there are also those who have more.

As Christians, we must feel led to share our blessings with the ones who have less. Furthermore, it should not bother us that others have more.

We must not sit in envy of them, for while they may have more of one thing or another, they also lack in some of the blessings we have. If we desire to have the blessings of others, we must also be willing to take on their problems. We all have enough problems of our own; we surely do not want theirs too.

Let us always be joyful at the Beautiful Loving Expressions and Sweet Surprises Initiated in the Name of God.

> *VERSE:* **Ephesians 1:3 (NLT)** *"All praise to God, the Father of our Lord Jesus Christ, who has blessed us with every spiritual blessing in the heavenly realms because we are united with Christ."*

Thoughts and Feelings:

_____

_____

_____

_____

_____

_____

_____

_____

_____

_____

DATE : _____

Chapter 29

God has blessed doctors with knowledge and ability to heal our bodies, but remember that Jesus is the Great Physician who heals body, mind and soul.

THE PROCEDURES THAT DOCTORS can do nowadays are amazing. Diseases or injuries that would have been fatal years ago, aside from divine intervention, are these days easily controlled, fixed, or cured. Physicians can go into many areas of expertise. Making it easy to find a skilled doctor for any ailment we may have. When we find a good doctor that is to our liking, we begin to place our trust in him or her. But, where does the trust we have for these doctors end and where does our faith in Jesus begin?

However good and skilled any doctor may be, not one of them can fix a troubled spirit, mend a broken heart, or piece back together a fractured soul. We all may have a testimony or two on how we or someone we know received a miraculous healing of the body through prayer and faith in Jesus Christ. We too can think of times when the peace that we receive from Jesus helped ease our cluttered minds. Without a doubt, the only way that our souls can be saved from sure death is to know Jesus is our Lord and Savior.

Some may ask, "If we have faith that Jesus can heal our bodies, then why do we go to the doctor?" My favorite answer is, "Because Jesus doesn't give work excuses." Doctors are blessed with skills and knowledge to heal our bodies and that is their purpose in this world, just as the Lord blesses his ministers to help heal our spirits.

Verse: **Luke 6: 18-19 (NLT)** *"They had come to hear him and to be healed of their diseases; and those troubled by evil spirits were healed. Everyone tried to touch him, because healing power went out from him, and he healed everyone."*

Thoughts and Feelings:

_____

_____

_____

_____

_____

_____

_____

_____

DATE _____

Chapter 30

As much as we wish the world revolved around us, the truth is that it revolves around the SON, Jesus Christ.

My wife, Melissa, used to sometimes tell me "Contrary to popular belief, Jeff, the world does not revolve around you!" When she said that, I would think, "Well, my world does." For me, it was about the way I felt about things, it was my opinion on various topics that mattered to me, and it was about my wants and needs. Oh boy! Was I wrong! God, and what he does, is not a part of our plans; we are a part of his plan, along with any and everybody who ever lived.

Our feelings, opinions, wants, and needs are important. They are important to God. God wants our feelings to be that of joy, peace, and love, for all the people he has placed in our lives. He wants our opinions to be that of the truth in all situations, whether it benefits us or not. To God, our wants and needs are also important and He will supply each of them accordingly. What we must do as Christians, is to fully and humbly accept the Grace of Jesus' sacrifice. We must look to, lean on, pray to, repent to, and always be mindful of Jesus Christ our Lord and Savior. We should look for Jesus in every aspect of our lives.

With Jesus at the very center of our lives and the very one with whom we place all our trust, we will be abundantly blessed. Our love will be warmer, our joy will be sweeter, our peace will be deeper, and our lives will be fuller of all the blessings the Lord our God has for us.

(The very center chapter and verse of the Holy Bible is Psalm 118:8) Who do we think God is trying to tell us the center of our own worlds should be?

Verse: **Psalm 118:8** *"It is better to trust in the LORD than to put confidence in man."*

Thoughts and Feelings:

_____

_____

_____

_____

_____

_____

_____

_____

DATE _____

Chapter 31

With wide-eyed wonder, look at what the Lord has for you next in life.

SOME OF THE MOST exciting times we can face in life are new beginnings. Going to new schools, new jobs, new cities, or new churches leads to feelings of wonder and uncertainty. When placed in new surroundings, our minds become filled with questions like, "Who will I meet, how will I find my way, will I be accepted, and was this the right decision?" But if we lay all these questions and uncertainty aside and realize that God has placed us in this new situation for a reason, then we will be filled with joy and wonder for the new journey ahead.

Discovering a world and a person in that world that we never knew existed pulls at our sense of adventure. Fresh new beginnings lead to learning about new people, new ideas, new experiences, and new sides to our self. When we look at these changes in life as a new assignment from God, then the feeling of fear and doubt can be easily overcome. Knowing that we do not face these new beginnings alone, for we always carry the Spirit of Jesus with us, all our anxiety can be washed away.

Just as the early Christians embraced the adventure of going to different cities to share the good news about Christ, we too must be excited at every new assignment the Lord gives us.

> *Verse:* **ACT 8: 4-5 (NLT)** *"But the believers who were scattered preached the Good News about Jesus wherever they went. Philip, for example, went to the city of Samaria and told the people there about the Messiah."*

Thoughts and Feelings:

_____

_____

_____

_____

_____

_____

_____

_____

_____

_____

DATE: _____

Chapter 32

Do the best you can with what God has given you. Others may find fault in you but the Lord will be pleased.

A TRUTH ABOUT LIFE IS that no matter what we do or how good we do it, someone will always find fault in it. This can be disheartening when we put our whole heart into accomplishing something good only to find someone trying to rain on our parade. How do we handle these moments when we are being persecuted for the good we do? Do the cheers of some drown out the booing of others? Can our ears only hear the praise or does our heart feel the pain of the complaints?

Ultimately when we use our God-given talents to further the Lord's kingdom, all the glory must go to God. All the hissing comes from that snake in the grass Satan, so it should not weigh on us in any way. Even if the world pats us on the back for a job well done, it should be the Lord that our hearts yearn to please.

When all is said and done, when all the cheers and boos have faded away, when all the riches that we accumulated are left for others to divide up, when the last handful of dirt is placed over our casket, and we are standing before the Lord, all we want to hear is, "Well done, my good and faithful servant." That statement and that alone must be the driving force behind all and everything we do.

> *VERSE*: **1 Peter 2: 19 (NLT)** *"For God is pleased with you when you do what you know is right and patiently endure unfair treatment."*

Thoughts and Feelings:

_____

_____

_____

_____

_____

_____

_____

_____

_____

_____

DATE: _____

Chapter 33

In life, walk with God, because if we run with the Devil we will surely fall.

THE BIBLE TELLS US of two men that walked with God. The first man was Enoch; the Bible says that Enoch walked in fellowship with God, and then Enoch disappeared because God took him. The second man was Noah; the Bible says that Noah was blameless and he walked in fellowship with God. We all know the rest of Noah's story and what God had tasked him with. Verses throughout the Bible tell us to walk in the ways of God by obeying His commands. What does it mean to walk with God? Can we be like Noah and Enoch and walk with God?

One of the most pleasant thoughts we can have is one day walking down the streets of Gold with Jesus by our side. Until that day comes, we will have to walk in our mind, heart, and soul in fellowship with God. The first step we can do to walk with God is to have Jesus be our model of love and compassion for all. We must also do like the Bible tells us and obey the Lord's commands to the very best of our ability. We must constantly be in prayer-- not meaning that we walk around all day with our heads bowed, but we should be in constant conversation, always looking for the

Lord in any and all situations. Another important step is leaning on God in situations that are too big, difficult, or emotional for us to handle on our own. We need to read the Lord's word daily; this will feed our starving souls. Trust and have faith that the Lord will deliver us from any problem, struggle or dilemma. Know with all our hearts that Jesus Christ is our Lord and Savior.

Running with the devil will offer promises of excitement and fun, but really only deliver heartache and may shorten the breaths we will take in life. Walking with the Lord will give us joy, peace, and love-- and we'll always have our best friend by our side.

> *Verse:* **Deuteronomy 30: 16-18 (NLT)** *"For I command you this day to love the Lord your God and to keep his commands, decrees, and regulations by walking in his ways. If you do this, you will live and multiply, and the Lord your God will bless you and the land you are about to enter and occupy. But if your heart turns away and you refuse to listen, and if you are drawn away to serve and worship other gods, then I warn you now that you will certainly be destroyed. You will not live a long, good life in the land you are crossing the Jordan to occupy"*

Thoughts and Feelings:

_____

_____

_____

_____

_____

_____

DATE: _____

Chapter 34

With a joyful heart, help those around you, for God has placed you in their lives as a blessing to them.

THE OLD ADAGE THAT it is far better to give than receive rings loud and clear, especially when we give of ourselves. We all love to receive blessings, and I don't think that we would consciously turn one down. Yet, it is even better when we have the opportunity to be a blessing to someone else.

There is no better feeling than when we are used by God to be a blessing to someone else. Many times the blessing we can be is not us accomplishing a major task or job for someone, but at times we are merely an ear that listens, a hand that holds, two arms that hug or a smile that brightens some ones day. Whatever blessing we are to be to someone, it is very important that we do whatever it is with joy in our heart.

When we are sent to listen, we are not to look at the clock and say, "It's getting late." When we are the hand to hold, we are not to loosen our grip until we have completely pulled our friend up to safety. When we are the arms that hug, we are not to let go until our brother or sister can stand on his or her own two feet. When we are the smile, we are to smile and glow always with the joy that the Lord has placed in our hearts. When we are a blessing to someone else, the greater joy will be felt by us for knowing that the used us as a showing of his love.

VERSE: **Hebrews 13: 16 (NLT** *"And don't forget to do good and to share with those in need. These are the sacrifices that please God."*

Thoughts and Feelings:

_____

_____

_____

_____

_____

_____

_____

_____

_____

_____

_____

DATE: _____

Chapter 35

No matter how bad the pains in life are, be thankful we have Jesus to help us through and have faith that, someday soon, all will be well.

WHETHER WE ARE SUFFERING from physical pain, emotional pain, or spiritual pain, there is someone who can help. Whether it is a sharp pain, a constant ache or chronic pain that never goes away, there is someone who can help.

I went to my back doctor this week and he told me that I will most likely have pain with my back forever, but hopefully through physical therapy and taking pain medicine, we can make it tolerable." What he told me really didn't sink in until later that evening and the next morning. I could forever be in misery with this pain. I may always have this pain that prevents me from having any type of normal life. I may always have this pain that prevents me from being able to do many of the things that I love to do. Then God spoke, telling me, "though you may have to deal with pain now, your future is in my hands and someday all will be well."

I know that with the love and peace that I have in Jesus, I can endure for now; and with the compassion from Jesus, someday I will be healed.

The Lord loves us, though it may be difficult to feel that when we are in some type of pain. When we stay true in our faith in Jesus, we can make it over the tough times and will have our day in the sun where all will be well.

> *Verse:* **Romans 8: 35-37 (NLT)** *"Can anything ever separate us from Christ's love? Does it mean he no longer loves us if we have trouble or calamity, or are persecuted, or hungry, or destitute, or in danger, or threatened with death? (As the Scriptures say, "For your sake we are killed every day; we are being slaughtered like sheep.") No, despite all these things, overwhelming victory is ours through Christ, who loved us.*

Thoughts and feelings:

_____

_____

_____

_____

_____

_____

_____

_____

_____

_____

_____

_____

_____

_____

DATE: _____

Photo by William Lee

Chapter 36

How do we celebrate our success? Do we pat ourselves on the back or do we give the glory to God, who made it all possible?

HOW MANY BOOKS OR programs offer us the secrets on how to succeed in life? There are books and programs on how to be a successful sales person, how to be a successful leader, how to be a successful parent, etc. Well, I would be remiss if I didn't offer in this book a 10-step process on how to be a successful Christian.

10 Steps on How to Be a Successful Christian

1. Know Jesus Christ as our Lord and Savior.

2. Read God's word "The Holy Bible" every day.

3. Pray constantly.

4. Have fellowship with other Christians.

5. Show the Spirit of Jesus in us through
    our words and actions.

6. Reach out to others and help them to
    know Jesus as their Savior.

7. Have faith and trust in God in all situations.

8. Lean on God when the going gets tough.

9. Look to God for guidance when we don't know what to do.

10. Be humble and give all the thanks and glory
    to God for any and all success we have.

Whether we use of our God-given talents, or through our prayers, or our faith in God that all is possible, whatever leads to our success in life, let us always make sure to give all the honor and glory to Him who made it possible, Our Lord Jesus Christ.

> *Verse:* **2 Timothy 2: 15 (NLT)** *"Work hard so you can present yourself to God and receive his approval. Be a good worker, one who does not need to be ashamed and who correctly explains the word of truth."*

Thoughts and Feelings:

_____

_____

_____

_____

DATE: _____

Chapter 37

Through the Grace, Power and Love we have in Jesus. ALL is POSSIBLE!

IMMEDIATELY WHAT POPS INTO my head is the song from the late 60s, "To Dream the Impossible Dream." With our faith in Jesus, we can dream that impossible dream, we can achieve that impossible goal, and we can expect that impossible miracle!

Through the Grace that we have in Jesus, our most horrible past sins can and will be forgiven if we repent from the bottom of our souls. Through the power of Jesus, diseases can be healed, mountains can be moved, and lives will be changed. Through the Love of Jesus, all tears are dried, all heartaches disappear, and new relationships and friendships are formed that benefit all.

Through the Lord our God, ANYTHING is Possible. We can all be empowered with Jesus' Holy Spirit to accomplish many great and wonderful things in his name. We can all be at a peace knowing that, through Jesus, there is never a hopeless moment that we ever have to worry about. So with Jesus, let us all dream the Possible, dream.

Verse: **Jude 1: 25 (NLT)** *"All glory to him who alone is God, our Savior through Jesus Christ our Lord. All glory, majesty, power, and authority are his before all time, and in the present, and beyond all time! Amen."*

Thoughts and Feelings:

_____

_____

_____

_____

_____

_____

_____

_____

_____

_____

_____

_____

DATE: _____

Chapter 38

Do a kind act for someone today without expecting anything in return--not even a blessing--for in Jesus we are already oh so very blessed.

EVERY DAY WE ARE afforded many opportunities to do something kind for someone. It could be a big life-changing act or a simple thing that makes that person's day a little easier, a little brighter, and a lot more blessed. Whether the kindness we share is something big or a simple, yet significant, both show the Spirit of the Lord in us.

If all we gain for our efforts is someone seeing the Spirit of Jesus in us, then we have already received the prize for our efforts. Knowing Jesus as our Lord and Savior and the wonderful Grace he gives us is the greatest gift that we can ever receive. "Paying it forward" is the new catch phrase and concept, but it really is not new at all, for Jesus tells us in Matthew 7: 12 "Do to others whatever you would like them to do to you…" When we remember this teaching, doing kind things for others makes perfect sense, for that is how we want to be treated.

This kindness we show should come with some kind of warning label though. For the more kind and caring things we do for others, the more we will desire to do. We will also find ourselves feeling bad when we let the opportunity to be kind pass by.

God bless you, brothers and sisters, may Jesus' Spirit of kindness shine out of all of us today and forever for the whole world to see.

> *Verse:* **Acts 20: 35 (NLT)** *"And I have been a constant example of how you can help those in need by working hard. You should remember the words of the Lord Jesus: 'It is more blessed to give than to receive.'"*

Thoughts and Feelings:

_____

_____

_____

_____

_____

_____

_____

_____

_____

_____

DATE: _____

Chapter 39

Behind every gray cloud there is a blue sky; behind every problem there is a blessing from God.

I REMEMBER THE VERY DAY the Lord gave me this message. I had accompanied my wife to the dentist one morning. The day was gray and rainy. I knew that riding in a vehicle would cause more pain in my back, but I wanted to spend some time with my wife so I decided to go with her. On the 30- to 40- minute ride, we talked about many of the issues in our lives. We talked about the negative aspects of my back, her job and the kids. On our way home I stated that I wonder what the message was going to be for that day. Seconds later, we turned a corner and I looked up at the sky. In all the grayness of that day, there was an opening in the sky and the sun's rays were shining through. My eyes welled up with tears and I knew what the Lord was telling me.

Each person's life has many difficult challenges to face. We are always going to have issues in our lives that we will whine, cry, and moan about. With all the issues that we can worry about, it is easy for our minds to

get cloudy, preventing us from seeing all the blessings we have and all the blessings to come. We far too often forget just how blessed we are.

Let us always be mindful and embrace the challenges that life offers, for just as much as the flowers need the sunshine, they also need the gray cloud to bring the rain to help them grow.

> *Verse:* **Psalms 84: 6 (NLT)** *"When they walk through the Valley of Weeping, it will become a place of refreshing springs. The autumn rains will clothe it with blessings."*

Thoughts and Feelings:

_____

DATE: _____

Chapter 40

Remember: We don't tell God when; God tells us when.

WE ALL HAVE HEARD the statement, "God never places more on us than we can handle." That statement usually refers to when someone is facing a tough situation in life, but it rings true here also. Some of the blessings that the Lord has stored away for us are just waiting on us to possibly reach a higher level of maturity, understanding, or appreciation. Just as the prodigal son received his inheritance from his father early and then went and squandered it all away, we too might squander our inheritance if the Lord was to give all our blessings to us when we first wanted and asked for them.

Part of the Christmas fun is, knowing that we have gifts under the tree with our names on them. We sit and wonder with great anticipation at what they could be. We pick one up, look it over, rattle it a couple times, and set it down smiling, counting the days until Christmas morning. Then finally Christmas morning arrives. As we start to open our gift, our stomachs jump with excitement and our minds race at what it could be. When the last piece of wrapping paper is thrown to the side and we fling open the box to reveal the perfect gift, joy glows across our face. Then we utter those famous words "It is just what I always wanted! How did you know?" It is the same way with our blessings, God knows! God knows the perfect blessing we need and exactly when we need it.

We all know that the Lord has many blessings for us to come. While our patience is tested, we must understand that God knows what and when things will bless us the most.

Verse: **1 Peter 5: 6 (NLT)** *"So humble yourselves under the mighty power of God, and at the right time he will lift you up in honor."*

Thoughts and Feelings:

_____

_____

_____

_____

_____

_____

_____

_____

_____

_____

DATE: _____

Chapter 41

God has a wonderful purpose for you, so embrace the process of becoming everything God wants you to be.

As an artist looks at a blank canvas, as a writer looks at a blank page, as a composer looks at the blank scales, and as a sculptor looks at an unshaped piece of clay, one thing they all have in common is that they have a purpose in mind. All these works they want to create will not be finished in a day. Their works may take a lifetime to complete making sure it is perfect without any flaws. The artists will be proud of their finished works, but will find the most satisfaction from the ups and downs of the process of creating these wonderful works of art.

We are God's blank canvas, blank page, blank scale, and unshaped piece of clay. The difference is that the blank and unshaped things that the artist's work on cannot feel the pain or enjoy the process like we can. How blessed we are, as we feel every stroke of the Lord's mighty brush as he paints the portrait of who we are. How wonderful it is to live the experiences as God writes the story of our lives. What a joy it is to sing songs of praise to God, as he creates the music in our lives that we dance to. How important it is to stand strong in our faith as the Lord knocks a chip off our shoulder with his mighty chisel to shape us into His vision of beauty and glory.

When God creates us, He has a vision of a beautiful work of art. He has a purpose for us. God wants us to display all His wonders and glory. The process of being all God wants us to be is filled with joy, pain, happiness, and sorrow. In the end, when we allow the Lord to work in our lives, it will be worth every step. Whatever we imagine we could be does not come close to the vision that God has for each one of us.

> *Verse:* **Acts 26: 16 (NLT)** *"Now get to your feet! For I have appeared to you to appoint you as my servant and witness. You are to tell the world what you have seen and what I will show you in the future."*

Thoughts and Feelings:

_____

_____

_____

_____

_____

_____

_____

_____

DATE: _____

Chapter 42

Through every twist and turn in life; through every sin then repenting; through every prayer prayed; through all, do we have a heart for God?

EVEN THOUGH WE DO our very best to stay on the straight and narrow, it can be difficult with all the many ups and downs, and twists and turns that life has to offer. We can get very frustrated when life feels out of control. Along with the rocky road that is our lives, the world throws many temptations our way. We do our very best to always do the right thing, but there are the times when... well, the times when we just don't. We all have prayed thousands of prayers, some big, some small, some important, and some maybe a little frivolous. In a day, we go to jobs, school, ball games, scout meetings; we make dinners, wash dishes, wash clothes, wash ourselves, get kids ready for bed, get ourselves ready for bed, go to sleep; then get up in the morning and do it all again.

Through all the uncertainty that life has to offer, our best plan is to set our hearts on the Lord and His ways. King David, who the Bible tells us was a man after God's own heart, had a life full of ups and downs. David was a young boy when he became a hero for slaying the mighty Goliath. He was then made to be a villain by King Saul and was forced to be on the run from the king and his soldiers. Then again, David was lifted to the status of hero as he became the King of Israel. King David next became a sinner by sleeping with another man's wife and setting up her husband to be killed. After realizing the error of his ways, David offered a very heartfelt repentance unto the Lord.

Throughout his days of being a hero, a villain and then a sinner, King David always looked to God for strength, wisdom, understanding, and forgiveness.

We too must have a heart for God. We must look to God for protection when life seems against us. We must look to God for guidance when we feel lost. We must talk to God in prayer always and from the heart. Also we must ask for His merciful forgiveness when we do wrong.

When we have a heart for God, we will surely be in His. In the good times and bad times in life, let us pray that God continues blessing us through it all.

Verse: Philippians 4: 11-13 (NLT) *"Not that I was ever in need, for I have learned how to be content with whatever I have. I know how to live on almost nothing or with everything. I have learned the secret of living in every situation, whether it is with a full stomach or empty, with plenty or little. For, I can do everything through Christ, who gives me strength."*

Thoughts and Feelings:

_____

_____

_____

_____

DATE: _____

Chapter 43

All Prayers must be followed with Faith that God will answer them.

ONE OF THE MOST exciting plays in football is nicknamed the "Hail Mary." This play is usually run when there are just seconds left in the game, the team that is losing has the ball around 50 yards away from the end zone and they need a touchdown to win the game. When the ball is snapped to the quarterback, all the receivers run to the end zone, and the quarterback heaves the ball all the way down to the receivers just hoping and praying that one of them catches it to win the game. Although usually not successful, there are times it has worked. So when a team is desperate, it is worth trying. The question we must ask ourselves, is this how we view prayer?

Do we look at praying to God as a last ditch effort for us to have a favorable outcome in whatever dilemma we may be going through? How many of us have said or heard someone say, "Well, the only thing left to do is pray." In even our most dire and desperate situation or even in the not-so-pressing issues, praying to God should be our first step. We must then follow up our prayers with the faith that the Lord will answer them.

If we think of our prayers as a roll of the dice, then we might as well save our time and not pray at all. Though our prayers may not always be answered when and exactly how we would like, we must always remember our Heavenly Father knows best. With praying being the first step we take in any situation, having faith that those prayers will be answered must always be step 1A.

My most heartfelt prayer is that we all grow closer in our relationship with Jesus Christ every day, through our prayers and our faith.

> *Verse*: **Mark 11: 22-24 (NLT)** *"Then Jesus said to the disciples,*
> *"Have faith in God. I tell you the truth, you can say to this*
> *mountain, 'May you be lifted up and thrown into the sea,' and*
> *it will happen. But you must really believe it will happen and*
> *have no doubt in your heart. I tell you, you can pray for anything,*
> *and if you believe that you've received it, it will be yours."*

Thoughts and Feelings:

_____

_____

_____

_____

_____

_____

_____

DATE: _____

Chapter 44

When we are (G)uilty of sin, we must (R) epent, to gain (A)tonement, through (C) hrist so we may (E)nter heaven. (GRACE)

WITHOUT GOD'S GIFT OF Grace what would be our eternal future? Could we be good enough to earn our way into Heaven? How many bulls, lambs and doves would have to be sacrificed to pay the debt for our sin? I am sure we all can guess what the answers would be to these questions. God knows these answers also.

God loves us and wants us to be with Him for eternity, so He gave us the wonderful gift of grace. The truth is we are all guilty of some sin. We do our best to hide our sin from others but we cannot hide our sin from God. When we are guilty of committing these sins, no matter how big or how small, we must humbly repent and ask for forgiveness. By repenting of our sins, we can gain the atonement we need to spend eternity with the Lord. What a sacrifice it was that Jesus Christ made for each one of us on the cross. He paid the price for the sins that each one of us commits. Because of the wonderful gift of Grace, one day we can walk through the gates of Heaven. The only price we have to pay is with our faith and believing in

Jesus Christ as our Lord and Savior. How odd it is though that there are still some that have not accepted and will not accept the wonderful free gift of Grace. We must be ever vigilant to try and share the gift of grace with anyone we can.

As Christians, we all have many wonderful things to be thankful for and it all begins with one great and wonderful gift, grace. Let us be forever thankful for the wonderful gift of Grace the Lord gives us and let us never hesitate to share it with any and every one we meet.

Verse: **Ephesians 1: 6-7 (NLT)** *"So we praise God for the glorious grace he has poured out on us who belong to his dear Son. He is so rich in kindness and grace that he purchased our freedom with the blood of his Son and forgave our sins."*

Thoughts and Feelings:

_____

_____

_____

_____

_____

_____

_____

_____

_____

DATE: _____

Chapter 45

A strong body can be broken but a soul that is strong in the Lord only gets stronger through faith, no matter what the world throws against it.

WHAT IS THE TRUE measure of a person's strength? Is their strength measured in the amount of weight they can lift, the endurance they have to keep going, or their ability to withstand physical pain? To build physical strength, many hours must be spent in a gym or on a track. But is physical prowess the truest measure of strength?

One of the strongest people I know is 90 years old. She weighs 98 lbs. and has trouble with her eyes. Obviously she is not physically intimidating. Rather her strength is her spirit, in her soul, and in her faith in God. Her name is Lillian Gray and she has endured many life shattering, faith rattling, soul wrenching things in her life.

Thirty years ago, three of Lillian's sons were off shore working on a shrimp boat, just like they had done many times before. When it came time for them to be home, they never arrived. The initial thought was that maybe they had car trouble and they would be home soon. But after hours of waiting, Lillian went to go find her boys. Their vehicle was still where it was parked that morning and, frightfully, the boat they were on that day was not at the pier. Dread and fear gripped Lillian as she began to really become worried. She called anyone she could think of that might know where her sons were. The rest of that night was filled with many trips up and down the beach with eyes fixed out on the Gulf, just looking for any sign of boat lights. Her eyes strained searching and hoping. She was steadily praying for any sign of her boys. After the veil of darkness was lifted, there was still no sign of the boat or, sadly, of her sons. To this day there has never been any sign or any clue at what may have happened to her sons. Still her faith in the Lord remained strong. Twenty five years later, she lost another son to an unexpected heart attack. I remember her devastation, but I was also amazed at her strength. Her husband has passed on as well as her brothers and sisters, but there is no wavering in her faith. During hurricane Katrina everything she owned, including her house, was washed away into the Gulf of Mexico. All the possessions that were reminders of her children, her husband and other family members were gone. She had to sleep on blowup mattresses at the church. She then got a FEMA trailer, (which made her sick). Next was a move to a single-wide trailer with her son and his family who also lost everything. Then the Lords blessings arrived. She was blessed with a house built by the goodness and charity of others. They also built a home for her son and his family. Through all these tragic events, she has never once lost her faith or her hope that she has in the Lord. She welcomes the comfort that she has in Jesus. She continues to pray every day. She continues to have faith in a better tomorrow. When the doctor tells her she is losing the sight in one of her eyes, she prays to God and chooses not to accept the Doctor's diagnosis. The only exercise she does to strengthen herself is to bow her head and put herself in God's mighty hands. One of her favorite songs is "I Can't Even Walk (Without You Holding My Hand)." She doesn't only listen to it, she lives it every day.

When Sister Lillian introduces me to people, she calls me her pastor, but it is her who has led me and taught me a new understanding of the strength of a person's soul and faith. Thank you and God bless you always, my dear friend Sister Lillian Gray.

Verse: **1 Peter 1:6-7 (NLT)** *"So be truly glad. There is wonderful joy ahead, even though you have to endure many trials for a little while. These trials will show that your faith is genuine. It is being tested as fire tests and purifies gold—though your faith is far more precious than mere gold. So when your faith remains strong through many trials, it will bring you much praise and glory and honor on the day when Jesus Christ is revealed to the whole world."*

Thoughts and Feelings:

_____

_____

_____

_____

_____

_____

_____

_____

_____

_____

_____

_____

DATE: _____

Photo by William Lee

Chapter 46

The Spirit of God keeps us cool when things get heated, keeps us warm when the world seems cold and shelters us when the rains of life fall.

THE WORLD CAN BE a big, mean, scary place that does whatever it can do to break us down. The world will do whatever it can to make us angry to the point we lose control. The world will make us feel cold and convince us that we are all alone and that no one cares. The world will beat and batter us to the point where all we want to do is sit down and cry or just give up altogether. But the only control that the world has over our emotions and feelings is the control that we give it. Satan knows exactly what makes us angry. He knows how to make us feel lonely. Satan does everything he can to try and break us down. But as Christians, we serve and worship our God who keeps us, loves us and protects us.

When we open ourselves to the Spirit of the Lord and let Him take control, then there is nothing that can be hurled at us to knock us down or make us even sway. When filled with the Spirit of the Lord, we can handle things that would usually make us mad. Being filled with the Spirit of the Lord means we are wrapped in His love which will keep us warm even on the coldest night. With the Spirit of God on our side, the world can throw whatever it wants at us, but we will endure to see brighter tomorrows.

Whatever comes our way today, let us just smile and thank the Lord for His wonderful comforting Spirit in our lives.

Verse: **2 Corinthians 6: 6-7 (NLT)** *"We prove ourselves by our purity, our understanding, our patience, our kindness, by the Holy Spirit within us, and by our sincere love. We faithfully preach the truth. God's power is working in us. We use the weapons of righteousness in the right hand for attack and the left hand for defense."*

Thoughts and Feelings:

_____

_____

_____

_____

_____

_____

_____

_____

_____

DATE: _____

Chapter 47

When in times of despair, do not throw our hands up in surrender, but instead throw our hands up inviting Jesus to lead us to victory.

S OMETIMES IN LIFE, IT seems like there is no hope. At times, all we feel like doing is giving up. When we are battered and beaten, we might want to throw our hands up in the air and say, "enough is enough, I Quit!" But when we have faith in Jesus, there is always hope. With Jesus, we can stand strong against whatever dilemma we are facing. With our faith in Jesus Christ, we can keep our head up knowing that we shall overcome and will be able to throw our hands up in victory.

This all sounds nice and simple, but the reality is, it can be very frustrating when dealing with extremely stubborn people, or situations that are far too big for us to handle. Moses could have been very frustrated with the Pharaoh when his cold heart was hardened against Moses' requests, but Moses just faithfully called upon the Lord for guidance. Finally Moses' faith and persistence was rewarded with the release of the Hebrews. Before too long though, Moses was faced with another dilemma: thousands of whining Hebrews all around him, chariots charging toward him and a huge deep sea in front of him. Again Moses called upon the Lord for guidance and deliverance. The Lord told him to raise his hand above the sea, and when he did, the waters parted and the Hebrews walked to safety.

When in times of great despair, Moses continued to always look and call on the Lord. We too must take the same approach to all the frustrating things we will encounter in life. We must always look to Jesus and His ways so we may call on His Holy name. Let Him lead us so we will be able to throw our hands up in mighty victory.

Verse: **John 16: 33 (NLT)** *"I have told you all this so that you may have peace in me. Here on earth you will have many trials and sorrows. But take heart, because I have overcome the world.""*

Thoughts and Feelings:

_____

_____

_____

_____

_____

_____

_____

_____

DATE: _____

Chapter 48

We may not always feel like smiling, but always be Joyous knowing that we are blessed and loved by God.

THERE ARE TIMES IN life when everything seems to go wrong. There are times when if there is something that can go wrong, it will. (This is also known as "Murphy's Law). They call it "Murphy's law," but how many of us have felt like it should be our name attached to this law. Along with our everyday dilemmas, we also have the tragic events and major physical ailments that wear on our happiness. It is hard to smile through tears and grimaces of pain. Even though there are a number of things that can make our lives difficult, not one of them makes the Lord love us any less. Through all our heart-wrenching issues, God still remains the same. No matter what we are going through, with Jesus we have hope of brighter tomorrows and an eternity in paradise.

What a tremendous testimony it is when, through all our troubles, we can stand tall and proclaim that we are blessed. How many people want to have that same hope, same joy, and same peace that we have in Jesus that keeps us going through every painful step of life? We must know that our lives are a gift from God. Know that for every problem we have, Jesus has a solution. Know that for every rough road we are on, Jesus will see us to the end. Know that for every diagnosis by a doctor, Jesus has the cure. What it all comes down to is that we can choose to sit around and stew in our own juices or we can choose to bask in the promises, the love, the hope, the joy, and the peace that we have in our Lord and Savior Jesus Christ.

> *Verse:* **Ephesians 1: 3-4 (NLT)** *"All praise to God, the Father of our Lord Jesus Christ, who has blessed us with every spiritual blessing in the heavenly realms because we are united with Christ. Even before he made the world, God loved us and chose us in Christ to be holy and without fault in his eyes."*

Thoughts and feeling:

_____

_____

_____

_____

_____

_____

_____

_____

_____

_____

DATE: _____

Chapter 49

Let us not worship God through tradition and ceremony, but worship the Lord humbly and on bended knee, utterly and completely from the heart.

WHEN WE PRAY AT night before we go to sleep, what does our prayer sound like? Does it sound like the same prayer we prayed the night before, and the night before that and the night before that? How many of us have our church's routine down to a science, knowing that after the offering, there's a 20 minute sermon, followed by the closing prayer and then we will be out of there in time to catch the big game. How many of us when attending church sit in the exact same pew we have sat in for years? How many of us would be in an uproar if our pastor changed the order of the service? For many people, church has become just a duty they are required to do for a couple hours a week. Please know I am not pointing fingers, for we all fall into this at times.

The problem with putting God and our worship of Him in the same old traditional and ceremonial box is that we deprive ourselves of a closer, more intimate relationship with Him. We deprive ourselves of many blessings that can only be received when we open the box and open ourselves to all that the Lord is and will be in our lives. Some of the most wonderful experiences we can have in life are when the Lord works in ways that are completely unexpected. When we worship the Lord through song, we must sing from the very depths of our souls. When worshiping the Lord in prayer, we must feel and own every word we pray.

When we truly give the Lord our most honest and heartfelt worship we will experience a more pure and powerful relationship with our Lord Jesus Christ.

Verses: **John 4: 23-24 (NLT)** *"But the time is coming—indeed it's here now—when true worshipers will worship the Father in spirit and in truth. The Father is looking for those who will worship him that way. For God is Spirit, so those who worship him must worship in spirit and in truth."*

Thoughts and feelings:

_____

_____

_____

_____

_____

_____

_____

_____

DATE: _____

Chapter 50

Have Faith in God and be ultimately at Peace.

WHAT PUTS US AT peace? What makes it so we can rest easy at night? Do the deadbolt locks on our doors give us peace? The only thing a lock does is keep an honest person honest. Do the insurance companies bring us peace with our car, house, medical and life insurance policies? The only peace gained from these is financial peace for the insurance companies themselves as they receive a huge amount of our paychecks every month. Do we gain peace listening to beautiful music, sitting in a bubble bath or taking a walk in the wilderness? Well our favorite albums all have a last song, bath water gets cold and eventually we have to come home. There is only one peace that puts our heart, mind and souls at ease and will last for an eternity and that is the ultimate peace we have when we place our faith in Jesus Christ our Lord.

Quiet moments of prayer can calm a troubled heart. Prayers offered in the middle of the storms of life will calm the raging winds. Giving our cares, worries and problems to our savior Jesus Christ will relieve all the burdens on our souls.

Life is full of dramas and dilemmas that will try to steal away our peace. But, if we stay strong in our faith and true in our trusts, Jesus will sweep away everything that clutters our mind, heart, and soul, leaving us clear, peaceful skies to gaze upon.

Verse: **Romans 5: 1 (NLT)** *"Therefore, since we have been made right in God's sight by faith, we have peace with God because of what Jesus Christ our Lord has done for us."*

Thoughts and Feelings:

_____

_____

_____

_____

_____

_____

_____

_____

_____

_____

_____

_____

_____

_____

_____

_____

DATE: _____

Photo by William Lee

Chapter 51

The spirit of Jesus can be found when charity comes from the heart and true joy abounds.

WHY DO WE GIVE to charity? Do we give money to charity so we can get a bigger tax write-off at the end of year? Do we give so others can see how generous we are, so we can get a pat on the back? Do we give away our old and unused things so that we can go out and buy newer and better things? Do we give to charity because we deeply and truly care about our fellow man? I would hope we would all say truthfully the latter.

Giving should come from our hearts, without any reservations of the cost or the trouble. When we give, the only three that should know is they who receive it, us who give it and God who gave it to us to share. Whether we receive a blessing from God now or when we get to Heaven should not figure into our thought process at all. The joy that we will feel bringing a smile to some ones face is our payment in full.

We can learn many lessons from the way Jesus lived in his time here on earth and his teachings. As children, it was hard for us to understand the saying "It is better to give than to receive," but as adults and as Christians, this must resonate in the very depths of our souls.

> *Verse:* **Matthew 6: 1-4 (NLT)** *"Watch out! Don't do your good deeds publicly, to be admired by others, for you will lose the reward from your Father in heaven. When you give to someone in need, don't do as the hypocrites do—blowing trumpets in the synagogues and streets to call attention to their acts of charity! I tell you the truth, they have received all the reward they will ever get. But when you give to someone in need, don't let your left hand know what your right hand is doing. Give your gifts in private, and your Father, who sees everything, will reward you."*

Thoughts and Feelings:

_____

_____

_____

_____

_____

_____

_____

_____

_____

DATE: _____

Chapter 52

We all have sinned, so we must not judge each other; instead repent of our own sins and pray that we all live a life that is pleasing to God.

SIN IS DEFINED AS a transgression against moral or religious law. With that in mind, the sad truth is that we all are then law breakers. We all must agree with and accept the verse "all have sinned and have fallen short of the glory of God." I am sure that we can accept, even though we may not understand completely, that the Lord sees all sins equally, simply a sin is a sin is a sin. With the acceptance of these facts, it is still our human nature to point out, talk about, and pass judgment on the sins of others. The reasons for this run from making us feel better about our own sins to relief that the sins of others are brought out in the open while ours remain hidden. We must realize that our gossiping about and judging the sins of others is a sin also. While we do our best not to judge others, we must, whatever our sins are, repent of them to our Lord Jesus Christ. Repenting must be done from the heart humbly and truthfully. A great example of heartfelt repenting is Psalm 32, written by King David. Even more than our heartfelt repenting, we should strive daily to live a life that pleases God.

Instead of pointing out and gossiping about the sins of others, let us lift our brothers and sisters in prayer. Praying that they as well as us, would receive daily guidance and strength from the Holy Spirit, when being tempted by the world.

Verse: **James 4: 11 (NLT)** *"Don't speak evil against each other, dear brothers and sisters. If you criticize and judge each other, then you are criticizing and judging God's law. But your job is to obey the law, not to judge whether it applies to you."*

Thoughts and Feelings:

_____

_____

_____

_____

_____

_____

_____

_____

_____

_____

_____

_____

_____

_____

_____

_____

DATE: _____

Photo by William Lee

Chapter 53

Whatever is going on in our lives, always remember that all is good in the Lord

THERE ARE SO MANY things that go on in our lives every day. When at work during the day, we are forced to deal with a wide variety of stresses. We have stresses like trying to meeting job quotas or performing damage control when things go wrong. We may have to deal with an over-demanding boss, unproductive employees, or cutthroat co-workers. Then there is the drama of office politics and water cooler gossip. Who has the time or energy to deal with all this? After work, it is rushing our children to ball games and scout meetings. Making sure diner is cooked, homework is done, baths are taken, and teeth are brushed. Then it is making a budget plan, "robbing Peter to pay Paul" so the power doesn't get turned off, making sure laundry is done, lunches are made, then maybe off to bed to get up the next morning to do it all again. This doesn't leave a lot of time for God. But this is normal everyday life for many of us.

For the most part, we somehow make it all work. But what if some major event takes place? There are times when we have to handle layoffs, sicknesses, car troubles, house damages, and deaths. But through the everyday hustle and bustle of life to the catastrophic events, we must never, not even for a moment, lose sight of God. We must remain faithful knowing the Lord will give us strength to make it from day to day and will give us mercy to be able to handle the tragedies of life.

When we take time to look back over our lives and the busy times and the events that felt overwhelming back then, we will see how and when the Lord brought us through and made us a little wiser, a little stronger, and so very blessed. Never forget God is always good.

Verse: **Psalm 145: 8-9 (NLT)** *"The Lord is merciful and compassionate, slow to get angry and filled with unfailing love. The Lord is good to everyone. He shows compassion on all His creation."*

Thoughts and Feelings:

_____

_____

_____

_____

_____

_____

_____

_____

_____

DATE: _____

Chapter 54

God's help often comes in opportunities to help ourselves.

THERE IS AN OLD story that tells of a man who was stuck on the roof of his house as the flood waters were getting higher. He knelt there praying that the Lord would save him. Minutes later a man in a canoe came along and asked the man if he wanted to get in and be rescued. The man on the roof declined and boldly said, "No thank you, the Lord will rescue me." As the flood waters rose, the man had to climb higher on his roof and he continued to pray for the Lord to rescue him. Minutes later a man in a boat came along and asked the man if he wanted to get in the boat and be rescued. Again the man declined boldly stating that the Lord will surely rescue him, so the man in the boat left. A short time later, the flood waters were over the roof of the house and the man was hanging onto his chimney and praying for God to rescue him. Just before the waters went over the man's head, a helicopter came by and lowered a rope to him so he could be lifted to safety. Again the man declined the help, and with his last breath before being washed away, he shouted, "The Lord will rescue me." The next thing the man knew he was standing before God. He said to the

Lord "I prayed and prayed for you to rescue me but yet you never came and I drowned." God looked at the man with bewilderment and said, "I sent a canoe, a boat and a helicopter. What more did you want."

This story has stuck with me my whole life. The Lord has blessed each one of us with many talents to be able to survive and thrive in our world. God has blessed us with wonderful people to help us along the way. God has blessed us with many opportunities to have confidence in our God-given talents, lean on our loved ones, and to trust in the Lord. So when the flood water of life begin to rise let us make sure that we don't let our boat full of our blessings sail away without us.

> *Verse*: **Ephesians 5: 16-17 (NLT)** *"So be careful how you live. Don't live like fools, but like those who are wise. Make the most of every opportunity in these evil days. Don't act thoughtlessly, but understand what the Lord wants you to do."*

Thoughts and Feelings:

_____

_____

_____

_____

_____

_____

_____

_____

_____

DATE: _____

Chapter 55

My life is not perfect but still it is grand, Jesus is my savior and with him I stand.

WOULDN'T IT BE NICE if the moment we become a Christian, our lives become perfect? Just imagine the moment we get saved every ailment leaves our body, all heart ache is replaced by love, all our wallets or purses are filled with an endless supply of money, and all our hopes and dreams become reality.

As grand as that sounds, what we would lose by having everything we want is immeasurable. We would lose the tears of sadness and disappointment that help us grow as people. We would lose the pure joy of an unexpected blessing from God. We would lose the moments of feeling the Lord's peace and comfort when we must lean on Him for strength and understanding. We would lose the opportunity to show our faith in Jesus by standing strong in times of adversity. If our lives here on Earth were perfect, there would be no excitement in living them and the promise of Heaven would mean nothing to us.

The pain, sorrow, disappointment, and struggle must be embraced for they give us the special opportunity to lean on and stand tall in our faith in Jesus Christ. When we experience moments of perfection in our lives, we must cherish them, for these are few and far between. Love even more the times of imperfection in our lives, for the strength and mercy that Jesus gives us is the greatest showing of his love. Let us then smile in the face of adversity, for this shows the world that the Spirit of the Lord in us.

> *Verse*: **1 Peter 5: 10-11 (NLT)** *"In his kindness God called you to share in his eternal glory by means of Christ Jesus. So after you have suffered a little while, he will restore, support, and strengthen you, and he will place you on a firm foundation. All power to him forever! Amen."*

Thoughts and feelings:

_____

_____

_____

_____

_____

_____

_____

_____

_____

DATE: _____

Chapter 56

Set our sights on the things of Heaven, for it is better to look where we are going than where we have been.

W E COULD LOOK AT this whisper in two ways. One way could be that if we keep focusing on only the blessed days of the past, we may overlook the blessings of today and tomorrow. The other way is for us not to keep dwelling on past mistakes. If we repented of past sins, then in God's eyes we are forgiven. Rather we should focus our time and energy on what good we can do for others today and on the promises of Heaven tomorrow.

To set our sights on the things of Heaven is to have peace in the promise of God's wonderful gift of grace. It is to have the Spirit of Christ dwelling within us and showing this in our actions, and words we speak. To set our sights on the things of Heaven is to have a humble confidence in the Lord our God, that through our faith in him, all things are possible.

Longing for the good old days or carrying a grudge against someone or even ourselves accomplishes nothing, except risking a missed blessing of today or tomorrow. Whether we look at yesterday with great fondness or find ourselves cringing at past mistakes, know that when we walk with Jesus, there is always hope for a brighter today and blessed tomorrow.

> *Verse:* **Colossians 3: 1-3 (NLT)** *"Since you have been raised to new life with Christ, set your sights on the realities of heaven, where Christ sits in the place of honor at God's right hand. Think about the things of heaven, not the things of earth. For you died to this life, and your real life is hidden with Christ in God."*

Thoughts and Feelings:

_____

_____

_____

_____

_____

_____

_____

_____

_____

_____

DATE: _____

Chapter 57

When life feels out of control, the best way to regain control is to release all control to God.

THE SONG "JESUS TAKE the Wheel" by Carrie Underwood is a tremendous song and sentiment. Giving Jesus control of our lives truly is the very best action we can ever take. Simply stated, we are humans and we make mistakes; Jesus is our Lord and He is perfect. In whom would we rather leave our hopes, dreams, life, and future in, God or ourselves? There are times in our lives that just feel completely out of control. The more we try and fix the problem, the worse it gets. My wife and I went through a terribly tough time in our marriage some years back. For about a six-month period, life was completely out of control. Finally I prayed and told God I was tired of worrying about the problem and asked Him to do whatever He knew was best and let His will be done. From that moment on, it was like a huge weight was lifted off my shoulders and everything became easier and the path became clearer. It was not until I gave up complete control to God that everything became under control.

In all our stubbornness, we may sometimes find it difficult to give up control. This only leads to bigger problems for God to solve when we finally get smart and realize that it does ring true that our Heavenly "Father knows best."

Verse: **Psalms 143: 10 (NLT)** *"Teach me to do your will, for you are my God. May your gracious Spirit lead me forward on a firm footing."*

Thoughts and Feelings:

_____

_____

_____

_____

_____

_____

_____

_____

_____

_____

DATE: _____

Chapter 58

The time we spend in great struggle prepares us and leads to a time of great blessings from God.

L IFE CAN BE VERY difficult at times. While we usually can handle our daily dilemmas, sometimes we must face life-changing catastrophes. These can be things like physical ailments, career changes, deaths in the family and heart breaks. During these times, we can have feelings of despair and hopelessness. But it is in these times our faith in Jesus will keep us strong and give us hope for new opportunities and bigger blessings. Going through these times of great struggle will make it possible for us to fully understand and appreciate our future blessings.

When we learn to understand that God has a plan for us, we are more likely to find ourselves, strangely enough, embracing these tough times. A sad fact is that, for many of us, the only time we think about looking up to God is when we have reached rock bottom. For me, during these tough, painful times with my back, the understanding and knowing that ultimately God has a plan has helped me, rather lifted me up to where I can see that the road ahead is clear and full of wonderful blessings.

Let us embrace our struggles today with a smile, knowing God's plan is in place and soon there will be a wonderful blessing to follow.

Verse: **Zechariah 9: 12 (NLT)** *"Come back to the place of safety, all you prisoners who still have hope! I promise this very day that I will repay two blessings for each of your troubles."*

Thoughts and feelings:

_____

_____

_____

_____

_____

_____

_____

_____

_____

_____

DATE: _____

Chapter 59

Turn our problems over to God and let him make mole hills out of our mountains.

BLAME IT ON THE media or just our human nature, but we as humans tend to blow things way out of proportion. We take a small issue and start worrying about it, complaining about it, and then ask anyone we meet advice on how to fix it. Finally we attempt to fix the issue, usually with our emotion at an all-time high, so the little problem explodes into a national emergency. Okay maybe it doesn't get that out of control, but we do worry too much. We do exaggerate our problems to others for whatever reason and we do sometimes take bad advice and really mess things up. Yes, we make mountains out of our mole hills. But what if we turn the problem over to God?

No matter how big or small a problem, just ask, our Heavenly Father to do the wonders that he does, and let him fix it. God will give us the only surefire, tried and true, always perfect, never wrong, and ultimate answer to all our problems. When we turn to God for the answers and solutions to our problems we must have faith that the problem can and will be solved. The Lord will wipe away our tears and push away the clouds and remove any other thing that obstructs our view of the clear and correct solution. God's answers and solution may not be a quickest or the easiest fix, but it will be the right one.

Call it our human nature that when things are not quite right in our lives, we get worried, get nervous, and blow things way out of proportion. But when we walk daily with God and involve Him in our daily concerns, we can rest easy knowing that if Jesus is the Lord of our lives, then all our worries and problems will be swept away with one mighty swipe of the Lord's mighty hand.

Verse: **1 Peter 5: 7 (NLT)** *"Give all your worries cares to God, for he cares about you"*

Thoughts and Feelings:

_____

_____

_____

_____

_____

_____

_____

_____

_____

DATE: _____

Chapter 60

No matter what denomination we affiliate ourselves with, the only thing that matters is that we believe and trust in Jesus.

THERE IS ONLY ONE Bible, one God, one Savior, one faith, but oh so many denominations. Each denomination has each own set of guidelines, beliefs, and ways of doing things which is the denomination's doctrine. Denominations can give us a sense of belonging and a place where we can be with like-minded people of faith. We can go to a new town and look in a phone book and find a church of our denomination to attend and can be assured that the message and routine will be close to what we are used to. While there is much good natured ribbing amongst denominations, there is also likely some deep-seated distaste. There sometimes becomes a sense of feeling that the denomination we follow is the true doctrine and the others are risking their salvation unless they join us. While I will agree that there may be some sects whose teachings concern me for their followers, I am not going to put any denomination down if it helps someone find salvation in Jesus Christ. As Christians, it is not about which doctrine we

137

follow; it is first and foremost about being followers of Jesus Christ our Lord and Savior and having a personal relationship with Him.

One question I like to ask is, what denominations were the Disciples? Though each was his own man and they surely had their own opinions of God, one thing they all were, was followers of Jesus. The answer to the question is that they were born and raised in Judaism, but became the first Christians. They were just followers of Christ, Christians, nothing more, nothing less, not one a Catholic, not one a Baptist or not one a Methodist. They were just 100 % followers of Jesus Christ. That is what it boils down to for us also; it is not whether we are Pentecostal, Assembly of God or Lutheran, but are we one hundred percent followers of Jesus. We must not let doctrines outweigh the words in our Bible, we must not find ourselves worshipping our denominational leaders more than Christ and we must not let our denominations place limits on how God can manifest himself in us and what miraculous things he can do.

While belonging to one denomination or the other may give us a sense of comfort, let us not allow our church or denomination to become bigger than Our Lord Jesus Christ Himself.

> *Verse*: **Romans 15:5 (NLT)** *"May God, who gives this patience and encouragement, help you live in complete harmony with each other, as is fitting for followers of Christ Jesus."*

Thoughts and Feelings:

_____

_____

_____

_____

_____

DATE: _____

Chapter 61

Have faith in God. Have 100%, no doubt about it, written in stone, shouted from mountain tops, head held high, knowing in the Lord, FAITH!

B E BOLD IN OUR faith! Be strong and confident when sharing the good news of Jesus Christ. Do not ever deny knowing Jesus Christ as your Lord and Savior. Even in the face of extreme danger, stand tall and proud and proclaim your faith in Christ. Let us not just believe in Jesus but let us know in Jesus. Let our faith be heard in our voices when we speak of hope, trust, and love. Let our faith be seen on our faces with smiles of joy and eyes of mercy and peace. Let our faith be seen in our bodies with offering our arms to comfort, our hands to lift up, and our feet in going the extra mile for our brothers and sisters. Let our faith be in our action, in the charity we show, in the help we give, and in sharing the message of Jesus Christ.

With our faith so deeply in our hearts, we will find ourselves looking for God in everything in our lives. When miracles are needed, we will be wondering when, not if, His deliverance will come, because we know it will. We will feel a peace in our hearts knowing that God's plan is perfect and whatever we must endure, God has a reason.

Be bold, be strong, be confident, and be forever at peace in our faith in Jesus Christ our Lord.

> *Verse:* **2 Corinthians 4: 13 (NLT)** *"But we continue to preach because we have the same kind of faith the psalmist had when he said, "I believe in God so I spoke.""*

Thoughts and Feelings:

_____

_____

_____

_____

_____

_____

_____

_____

_____

_____

DATE: _____

Chapter 62

When the pains in life and battles of this world wear us down, let us find hope in the Lord and be refreshed in his Spirit.\

EXASPERATED-- WHAT A WORD, but a word that can define how we feel as we are battered and beaten like a small boat caught in a big storm on the sea of life. Physical pain can wear on us to the points of just about wanting to give up. Emotional pain can leave us tearing up and crying at any and everything. The constant daily battles we must face make us feel like we just want to go hide in a corner somewhere. With all these things that can and do erode away our joy, where can we find relief? Where can we regain some of that wonderful spirit that makes us, us?

There is a reason why we have church on Wednesday as well as Sunday. The mid-week services give us a few hours of relief, a few hours of recharging of our spirits. Reading God's word daily equips us with the necessary tools and inspiration to make our way from day to day. Being constantly in prayer gives us a balance when the things and events of our days attempt to knock us around. There is nothing that the world can attack us with that the Lord cannot make better when we give it to Him. With the hope we have in Jesus, the world can then go ahead and hit us with its best shot.

Through fellowship with our church families, through reading of God's word, and through constant prayer, we will be refreshed with God's Holy loving Spirit.

Verse: **Romans 15: 13 (NLT)** *"I pray that God, the source of hope, will fill you completely with joy and peace because you trust in Him. Then you will overflow with confident hope through the power of the Holy Spirit."*

Thoughts and Feelings:

_____

_____

_____

_____

_____

_____

_____

_____

_____

_____

DATE: _____

Chapter 63

We should not be defined by our location or those people around us; we should be defined by the spirit that dwells within us, and that is our Lord Jesus Christ.

WHETHER IT IS GUILT by association, geographical profiling, or racial profiling, labels are placed on people. People are also labeled by the clothes they wear, the shape of their bodies, the music they listen too, the words they use, their hair style, make up they apply, tattoos they have, and by the body parts they have pierced. There are so many things that one can use to label others; it is funny how often the labels are wrong or are disproved. The old saying "don't judge a book by its cover" is how we should look at each other.

All of us are from somewhere, live somewhere and are going somewhere. I grew up and lived in Northwest Montana for 19 years and now have lived in South Mississippi for 25 years. So am I a Northerner or a Southerner? A few times every year my sweet "Southern belle," wife will jokingly refer to me as a "Yankee" and my family in Montana tells me that I now talk funny with my southern drawl. What it all boils down to is that if we allow ourselves to judge and label people based on anything, we could be missing a blessing of making a new friend. Jesus loves everyone. He gave us the great commission to tell all nations and all people the Good News of the Christ. So if we feel that we must label someone, let us label each other as brothers and sisters in Christ and for the ones who have not yet found Christ, well, let's do our best to welcome them to the family by showing the spirit of Christ in us every day.

> *Verse:* **1 John 3: 24 (NLT)** *"Those who obey God's commandments remain in fellowship with Him, and He within them. And we know He lives in us because the Spirit He gave us lives in us."*

Thoughts and Feelings:

_____

_____

_____

_____

_____

_____

_____

_____

DATE: _____

Chapter 64

In a lifetime full of choices, choose God.

June 6, 1986 at 2:00 a.m., I chose Jesus Christ as my Lord and Savior. I am sure that most of you can recall the day you received your salvation. It is an important day in all our lives. It is the day that we were born again. We were made anew. It is the best choice of our lives, to be followers of Jesus. For most of us, tears of sorrow fell from our eyes while repenting of our sins, followed by tears of great joy when receiving Jesus' loving spirit. Tremendous feelings of peace, exhilaration, and freedom coursed through our bodies. For some it was an easy choice and for others it may have been a little more difficult. We must understand that choosing God does not end with our accepting Christ's salvation; that is only the beginning.

We as Christians must choose God every day, but don't fret; it's a good choice. When faced with temptations, it is up to us to choose God and resist. When waking up on Sunday morning, it is up to us to choose God, go to church and praise God, get a good message, and good fellowship. When we are antagonized, it is up to us to choose God and resist the desire to lash out.

For us to be blessed and known as one of God's chosen, it is only right that we choose God and his ways every day.

Verse: **Romans 6:16 (NLT)** *"Don't you realize that you become the slave of whatever you choose to obey. You can be a slave to sin, which leads to death, or you can choose to obey God, which leads to righteous living."*

Thoughts and Feelings:

_____

_____

_____

_____

_____

_____

_____

_____

_____

_____

_____

_____

DATE: _____

Chapter 65

It is not enough to read, hear and know God's word. God's words and ways must be applied to our daily lives.

I T IS VERY IMPORTANT that we feed on God's word daily. Whether we read his word for a few minutes or listen to the Bible on CD or listen to a message from a radio or TV minister, it is imperative that we spend time learning and getting closer to our Lord. It is not enough for us as Christians to just memorize a few key verses so that we at least we sound like we know what we are talking about. We must know the meaning of God's Word and let it speak to us and then apply it to our daily lives.

I used to coach in a Bible-based basketball league. At the end of the each season, the players would receive a special prize, like a basketball or backpack, if they memorized and could recite 12 selected Bible verses to the coach. With my teams, I didn't require them to memorize the verses, but what they had to do to earn their prize was tell me what the Bible verse meant and how it applied to their lives. I am pleased to say that my players always received the gift and most all accepted Jesus Christ as their Lord and Savior, during the season. For those that didn't at least the seed was planted. Now, I will admit that I was not much of a basketball coach and we lost most of our games, but more times than not, our teams defeated Satan and foiled his evil game plan.

I fully believe that the Holy Bible is alive with the Spirit of the Lord and we must allow it to speak to us and then allow it to come alive through every action in our daily lives.

> *Verse*: **Philemon 1: 6 (NLT)** *"And I am praying that you will put into action the generosity that comes from your faith as you understand and experience all the good things we have in Christ."*

Thoughts and Feeling:

_____

_____

_____

_____

_____

_____

_____

_____

_____

DATE: _____

Chapter 66

Though we may have stumbled in the past, today is a new day, so begin a fresh, new, joyous, peaceful, passionate walk with Jesus.

ONE THING I THING I have understood, preached and taught is that we should dedicate each new day in growing, walking and loving the Lord. When a person boldly says that he or she is going to dedicate their life to the Lord and His ways, though noble, that person is already doomed to fail. No one, no matter how good and righteous he or she may be, can live a life without committing a sin. There will be something that will angers or tempt them into thinking about--or possibly committing-- a sin. What if we break it down to living a day for the Lord? We may be able to accomplish that sometimes. But truthfully that may not even be possible either. The world is not a very nice place and the Devil does what he does to provoke us to anger, tempt us to sin and distract us from our walk with Jesus.

Praise the Lord that he knows we are only human and He understands there will times we will stumble and fall. That is why Jesus had to be sacrificed on the cross. He had to pay for our transgressions. We are so very blessed that Jesus loves us that much. He forgives us of our past sins we repent for and He will forgive us for the sins that we commit and then repent for today. We must understand though, that does not give us a license to sin.

When we face today and all the challenges it has in store for us, let us do our very best to passionately walk with Jesus and show the love, joy, and peace we have in him through our thoughts, words, and actions.

> *Verse:* **Titus 3: 4-5 (NLT)** *"But --- When God our Savior revealed His kindness and love, He saved us, not because of the righteous things we had done, but because of His mercy, He washed away our sins, giving us a new birth and new life through the Holy Spirit."*

Thoughts and Feelings:

_____

_____

_____

_____

_____

_____

_____

_____

DATE: _____

Chapter 67

The world may crumble around us, but we can stand firm on the rock that is our Lord Jesus Christ.

So MANY TRAGIC EVENTS can happen to us that can make us feel like our world is falling apart. The events of September 11, 2001 shook many Americans to the core. Hurricane Katrina in 2005 completely washed away everything that took many people a lifetime to build. The death of loved ones can make us not want to face the next day without them. Accidents that leave us only a shadow of our former selves can make us question our usefulness in this world. The loss of a job can leave us feeling hopeless and helpless when it comes to providing for our families. Many things can make us look ahead with tears of sadness and fear in our eyes, but when we stay strong in our faith, nothing should ever make us feel hopeless. In Jesus, there is always hope for a brighter tomorrow, a helping hand, a way to turn, and a shoulder to cry on.   On September 12, 2001, God saw to it that the sun rose and shone on the streets of New York City, and it has continued to shine in the days, weeks, months and years that have followed. God helped the people of New Orleans and South

Mississippi rebuild their lives after the storm. God sees to it that the fond memories of those passed can never die. If some of our abilities are taken away, God will bless us with new ways and new things we can do. When one door closes, God will then surely open a new one for us. With our faith in Jesus Christ, there is nothing that is too big, devastating, or heart wrenching that tomorrow cannot be faced with wide-eyed wonder.

May God bless each one of us on the many life-crumbling events that will happen in our lives, and let us set all of our faith, hope and dreams on our Lord Jesus Christ.

Verse: **Luke 6: 47-48 (NLT)** *"I will show you what it's like when someone comes to me, listens to my teachings, and then follows it. It is like a person building a house that digs deep and lays the foundation on solid rock. When flood waters rise and break against the house, it stands firm because it is well built."*

Thoughts and Feelings:

_____

_____

_____

_____

_____

_____

_____

_____

_____

_____

_____

_____

_____

_____

DATE: _____

Photo by William Lee

Chapter 68

Your smile and kind words can be the blessing that God sent to someone else.

WE ALL HAVE BAD days. It's not the day's fault. It just showed up as scheduled. But, it is the events, interactions, worries, attitudes and disappointments that take a perfectly good day and make it rotten. It is on these days that a smile from a stranger or a kind word could change our entire outlook for the day.

Smiling is so simple to do. It takes very little energy on our part but it can supercharge someone who is just running on fumes. A simple smile can change a normal, cold interaction into a warm conversation. When we follow up our smiles with kind words, we can create friendships.

When we tell someone to have a nice day and mean it, it is like offering a prayer to God, asking Him to help that person to have a good day. I myself have gotten into the habit of telling people, whether at the end of a phone conversation or an interaction in person, "God bless you." This startles some people, others return the blessing, and only a few have just said good bye. How we choose to interact with each other can make a big difference on how the rest of the day may turn out.

We must keep in mind that the Lord may and does use us, even when we are not aware, to deliver little day-changing blessings, wrapped up in our smiles.

Finally I would like to say, God bless you and have a very wonderful and blessed day!

Verse: **1 Peter 3: 8-9 (NLT)** *"Finally, all of you should be of one mind, sympathizing with each other. Love each other as brothers and sisters. Be tenderhearted, and keep a humble attitude. Don't repay evil for evil. Don't retaliate with insults when people insult you. Instead, pay them back with a blessing. That is what God has called you to do, and he will bless you for it."*

Thoughts and Feelings:

_____

_____

_____

_____

_____

_____

_____

_____

_____

DATE: _____

Chapter 69

As God molds us into who he wants us to be, some of the most painful times are when we stubbornly hold onto things we really do not need.

WHETHER IT IS PLAY-DOUGH or actual pottery clay, at some point in our lives, we have had an opportunity to mold a lump of clay into something. As we sit there and look at the clay, our minds begin to race with ideas of what we cold mold it into. While it takes some skill to mold a perfectly round bowl, even an inexperienced and unskilled person can mold the clay into a rough shape of a bowl. What if the lump of clay we were to use had a stick in the middle of it and no matter how hard we tried, we couldn't get the stick out without leaving a good bit of the clay on the stick. That would make it a lot harder to mold the clay into the right shape and size. Now what if the clay had dirt and sand mixed in it and of course nothing we could do would remove all of the grit. It would be impossible to make a bowl that was perfect even with the most skilled hands. This is how it is when God tries to mold us into who He wants us to be when we become reborn in Christ.

While He tries to change the way we talk and react with others, we may stubbornly hold onto our old ways of communicating. While He looks for a commitment from us, we refuse to give up our addiction and desire to keep doing what we did as the old us. There are many personal examples that each of us could give from our own lives of hanging onto the old us. While it is sometimes painful to give up the things that governed over the old us, the joy and peace we have in the Lord is worth any amount of discomfort as God molds us into the perfect vessels that can be filled with His Holy Spirit and pour out on all.

> *Verse*: **1 Peter 1: 14 (NLT)** *"So you must live as God's obedient children. Don't slip back in your old ways of living to satisfy your own desires. You didn't know any better then."*

Thoughts and feelings:

_____

_____

_____

_____

_____

_____

_____

_____

DATE: _____

Chapter 70

The Lord gives us strength to accomplish anything.

WE ALREADY TOUCHED ON this in earlier whispers, but it is very important for us to understand and fully believe this. Many times in life, situations and dilemmas seem hopeless. There are obstacles that stand in our way that try to prevent us from reaching our goals and becoming all that the Lord wants us to be. These obstacles seem so much bigger than we are, which tends to make us lose our focus on the task at hand. Along with the challenges we face, the shear length and time of the journey can also get the better of us. Whatever we face, we must keep our rock-solid faith in God.

Let us always take heart and never forget that we are not alone on our journey, for when we walk in the ways of the Lord, we do not walk alone. When we carry the Lord with us, there will be no load too heavy for us to bear, for we will not bear the load alone. When we allow ourselves to be lifted by the Lord's spirit, there will be no mountain too high for us to climb.

We all will face challenges in our lives. While these challenges may seem insurmountable, there is nothing that, with our faith in the Lord our God, we cannot handle, survive and thrive from.

> *Verse:* **Psalm 46: 1 (NLT)** *"God is our refuge and strength, always ready to help in times of trouble."*

Thoughts and feelings:

_____

_____

_____

_____

_____

_____

_____

_____

_____

_____

_____

DATE: _____

Chapter 71

JESUS... (Enough said)

J ESUS-- THERE IS NO other name that is more known throughout the world and invokes so much passion. As small children, we were sung to and told that Jesus loves us. When we reached the age of understanding many of us accept Jesus as our Lord and Savior, but it might have taken awhile longer for others.

Whatever age we are when we give our lives to Jesus, immediately, our knowledge, understanding and relationship with Him changes. Jesus stops being a historical figure in books and depicted in movies. He then becomes our Heavenly Father, our Lord, our Savior, our King, our best friend, and our one and only. Jesus is the answer to all of the tough questions in life. Where do we turn for help with our problem? Jesus. How will we find peace in the gut-wrenching times in life? Jesus. How shall we overcome? Jesus! Jesus! Jesus is the Answer.

Each one of us is blessed with our own personal relationship with Jesus. Each one of our relationships with Jesus is as different as we are. Not one of them is more right than the other, just as long as in our hearts we know that Jesus is our Lord. It is especially important that we do not try to sit and judge others relationship with Jesus. Jesus Christ walked the earth over 2000 years ago teaching, healing, loving, and ministering. Today through reading God's word, through prayer and through our daily walk, Jesus is still teaching, healing, loving, and ministering to each of us. While his greatest gift is the sacrifice he made on the cross, He still gives us many wonderful blessing every day.

My hope and prayer is that we all continue to grow closer to Jesus every day.

Verse: **John 14: 6 (NLT)** *"Jesus told him, "I am the way, the truth and the life. No one can come to the Father except through me.""*

Thoughts and Feelings:

_____

_____

_____

_____

_____

_____

_____

_____

_____

_____

DATE: _____

Chapter 72

Little blessings that come and go is God's way of preparing us for the Greater blessing we have in store.

WHETHER WE THINK OF past blessings as lessons learned or that the blessing had run its course, not all blessings are permanent. One blessing helps us grow in maturity for the next blessing to come. It is just like climbing a ladder: we can't step on the fifth step until we have stepped on step one, two, three and four. God is wise; He knows that until we reach certain levels of understanding, the bigger blessings would be wasted.

If we were to take time to look over our past, we would clearly see that one blessing led to another and then another and so on. People that the Lord places in our lives to help us along our journey will lead us to others who will help us keep the path that God needs us on. Just as we are not to dwell on past sins that we repented for, we also are not to mourn blessings that have come and gone, lest we miss the next one.

Let us always be appreciative of every blessing God gives us and let us always be alert for our many blessings that are soon to come.

Verse: **Luke 16: 10 (NLT)** *"If you are faithful in little things, you will be faithful in large ones. But if you are dishonest in little things, you won't be honest with greater responsibilities."*

Thoughts and Feelings:

_____

_____

_____

_____

_____

_____

_____

_____

_____

_____

_____

DATE: _____

Chapter 73

Put down our umbrellas. Let the Holy Spirit rain down upon us and saturate our souls, washing away the rust so that we can shine for the Lord.

I LOVE TO WATCH THE rain; the harder it rains the better. It is exhilarating yet relaxing. Furthermore, in the right circumstances, I don't mind being caught in it without an umbrella. The first few drops that hit are uncomfortable to the point where they almost sting. As my clothes and hair start getting saturated, there becomes an acceptance of the drenching down pour-- not a discontent acceptance, but one of, this is just the way it is. When every stitch of my clothes and every strand of my hair and every inch of my body are totally saturated with the shower from the heavens, I begin to crave for more and more of the moist drops. As the rain slows and then stops, I feel a yearning for more of what the heavens have to offer. After arriving home, the clothes are peeled from the body and there is a cleansed feeling that reaches the soul. The warm shower that follows almost cheapens the whole experience.

This same thing can be felt when we open ourselves completely and allow God's Holy Spirit to rain down on us. There are feelings of discomfort when we throw aside our inhibitions and allow the Holy Spirit to take us to a full and pure worship of the Lord. As the Spirit starts to saturate our every thought and feeling, we become completely and utterly submissive to where God leads. Soon we crave the pure loving feeling of the Holy Spirit. There is a sense of cleansing throughout our entire soul; all our problems, worries and past mistakes are washed away and we become shining beacons from which God's light glows.

We far too often hold back on the way we want to worship God for fear of what others may think of us. But we must always remember that on our day of reckoning the only opinion that counts is that of our Lord.

Verse: **Acts 1: 8 (NLT)** *"But you will receive power when the Holy Spirit comes upon you. And you will be my witnesses, telling people about me everywhere---in Jerusalem, throughout Judea, in Samaria, and to the ends of the earth."*

Thoughts and feelings:

_____

_____

_____

_____

_____

_____

_____

DATE: _____

Chapter 74

Joyfully give of our time, money and self, expecting nothing in return, for God loves a cheerful giver and that is blessing enough.

WHILE SOME OF US would gladly give a few hours to help the community and offer ideas to improve the neighborhood, when it comes to money, we suddenly turn into Scrooge himself (bah humbug). There are those who would generously open their wallets and pocket books and dole out some cash, but when it comes to getting involved, it is a big no thank you. Whatever type of person we are, none less or more valuable, it is imperative that we happily give for the betterment of others.

God blesses each one of us with our own abundances, whether it is knowledge, leadership, organization, teaching, helping, or money. As Christians, we must have, at the core of our souls, a need to bless others with what our Lord has blessed us with. However, we must not look for recognition, praise, applause or anything else in return. God will take care of delivering the Blessings that we have coming.

As we go throughout our day, let us look for and seek out ways to help and ways to be a blessing to those who intersect our lives. God Bless.

Verse: **2 Corinthians 9: 7 (NLT)** *"You must each decide in your heart how much to give. And don't give reluctantly or in response to pressure. "For God loves a person who gives cheerfully.""*

Thoughts and Feeling:

_____

_____

_____

_____

_____

_____

_____

_____

_____

_____

_____

_____

DATE: _____

Chapter 75

I will gladly crawl many miles down a dusty road with Jesus in my heart, to someday walk down the streets of gold with Jesus by my side.

IT CAN BE VERY frustrating to see people who deny and renounce Christ yet are very successful and wealthy. We wonder why should they, be so well off while we struggle pay check to pay check; we are the ones who believe in and love Jesus. We get frustrated that others receive awards and accolades in what they do while we are just counted as a number and our efforts go unnoticed. If these are some of the thoughts that we struggle with, we must step back and get back in God's word, lest we may even miss out on our own streets of gold.

As Christians, it is not about what others own, but what our Lord has blessed us with and using it to bless others. As humble servants of Jesus, we are not to wait for, expect or long for a pat on the back for all we do. There is no amount of money or no award that can even bring as much joy to our lives as the feeling we have with our Lord and Savior in our hearts. The knowledge of knowing that one day we shall begin our walk for eternity with Jesus Christ in Heaven is the best comfort and security that we need. True happiness is not in what fills our trophy cabinets; it is not in what is in our wallets and bank accounts; but it is in who lives in us and the spirit that pours out of our hearts, Our Lord and Savior Jesus Christ.

In our human nature, there will be times in which envy and jealousy creep in, but let us be quick to remember that there is no amount of treasure on earth that can equal the treasure we have stored away in Heaven.

> *Verse:* **Hebrews 10: 22-23 (NLT)** *"let us go right into the presence of God with sincere hearts fully trusting Him. For our guilty consciences have been sprinkled with Christ's blood to make us clean and our bodies have been washed with pure water. Let us hold tightly without wavering to the hope we affirm, for God can be trusted to keep His promise."*

Thoughts and Feelings:

_____

_____

_____

_____

_____

_____

_____

_____

DATE: _____

Conclusion

I HOPE AND PRAY THIS book was a blessing to you over the past 75 days or so. I hope it helped you in your daily walk with the Lord and you have shared and will share it with others. God has blessed each one of us with a wonderful life. Let us make the best of it by walking closer with Jesus every day, by reading the Bible daily, sharing the awesome gift of Grace with others, praying constantly, and always being mindful of the Lords grand plan for our lives. I pray we all open our hearts, minds and souls to any and every thing the Lord has for us. Please look for Volume 2 that should be out soon. I will welcome any feedback you would like to give. May God bless you abundantly always and forever, Amen.

Jeff Odell

Biography:

J EFF WAS BORN AND raised in Missoula Montana. His father, Wes Odell, was a mechanic at the local paper mills. He passed away in 1988. Jeff's mother is Florence Viktora, she has been a waitress at several different restaurants in Missoula and now works at the local Wal-Mart. Jeff has one brother Brad, who works at a tire shop in Missoula. Jeff grew up in a good home, though they never attended any church, but there was an unquestioned belief in Jesus. On June 6th, 1986 at 2:00 am, Jeff accepted Jesus Christ as his Lord and Savior. Later that day Jeff reported to Navy boot camp in San Diego California. Jeff served 4 years in the U.S. Navy. While in the Navy Jeff met his wife Melissa (Missy) Evans. Upon leaving the Navy Jeff and Melissa made a home in Vancleave Mississippi where they raised 3 children. Melissa and Jeff have raised their children in a Christian home. The family has attended Mount Pleasant Methodist Church, First Baptist Church of Vancleave, where Jeff was licensed to the ministry in 2004. The family attended D'iberville Christian Assembly (DCA) where Jeff served as the youth minister and was ordained in 2006. While at DCA many of Jeff's youth accepted Jesus and were baptized. In September of 2006 Jeff felt called away to concentrate on Open Heart Ministry. In this time he has seen many lives changed by the power of the Holy Spirit and the daily Whispers from heaven. Though He suffered a back injury during this time which limits what He can do as a pastor, he has not slowed down in doing what he can to bring others to Christ. He tries in many ways to help other Christians have a closer walk with the Lord. Jeff has faith that when the Lord see fit, there will be a time when his back is healed. Jeff is always willing to share with anyone and everyone his love for our Lord Jesus Christ.

You can follow Jeff on twitter.
https://twitter.com/JeffreyOdell

For comments and questions on
the Whispers from Heaven, Jeff
can be contacted via e-mail at:
whisperfromheaven1@live.com

He can be contacted for
ministering and preaching at:
openheart4jesus@gmail.com
Jeff can also be reached via mail at:
Jeff Odell
P.O. box 5284
Vancleave, MS 39565